the
Women's Basketball Drill Book

WOMEN'S BASKETBALL COACHES ASSOCIATION

Betty Jaynes, Consultant
Beth Bass, CEO

Human Kinetics

Library of Congress Cataloging-in-Publication Data

The women's basketball drill book.
   p. cm.
  "A repackaging of the WBCA's Offensive basketball drills and the WBCA's Defensive basketball drills."
  ISBN-13: 978-0-7360-6846-8 (soft cover)
  ISBN-10: 0-7360-6846-5 (soft cover)
  1. Basketball for women. 2. Basketball for women--Coaching. 3. Basketball for women--Offense. 4. Basketball for women--Defense. I. WBCA's offensive basketball drills II. WBCA's defensive basketball drills III. Women's Basketball Coaches Association.
  GV886.W63 2007
  796.323'8--dc22

2007016325

ISBN-10: 0-7360-6846-5
ISBN-13: 978-0-7360-6846-8

Copyright © 2007 by Women's Basketball Coaches Association

Acquisitions Editor: Jana Hunter; **Developmental Editor:** Kevin Matz; **Assistant Editor:** Laura Koritz; **Copyeditor:** Annette Pierce; **Proofreader:** Sarah Wiseman; **Graphic Designer:** Robert Reuther; **Graphic Artist:** Tara Welsch; **Cover Designer:** Stuart Cartwright; **Photographers (interior):** chapters 1, 5, 6, 10, 12, 13, and 14 © Icon; chapters 2 and 3 © Human Kinetics; chapters 4, 7, 8, and 11 © Getty Images; chapters 9 and 15 © John Dunn/Icon SMI/Corbis; chapter 16 © Associated Press; **Photo Asset Manager:** Laura Fitch; **Photo Office Assistant:** Jason Allen; **Art Manager:** Kelly Hendren; **Associate Art Manager:** Alan L. Wilborn; **Illustrators:** Tammy Page, Tom Roberts, Sharon Smith, and Alan L. Wilborn; **Printer:** Sheridan Books

Printed in the United States of America   10 9 8 7 6 5 4 3 2 1

Human Kinetics
Web site: www.HumanKinetics.com

United States: Human Kinetics
P.O. Box 5076
Champaign, IL 61825-5076
800-747-4457
e-mail: humank@hkusa.com

Canada: Human Kinetics
475 Devonshire Road Unit 100
Windsor, ON N8Y 2L5
800-465-7301 (in Canada only)
e-mail: orders@hkcanada.com

Europe: Human Kinetics
107 Bradford Road
Stanningley
Leeds LS28 6AT, United Kingdom
+44 (0) 113 255 5665
e-mail: hk@hkeurope.com

Australia: Human Kinetics
57A Price Avenue
Lower Mitcham, South Australia 5062
08 8372 0999
e-mail: info@hkaustralia.com

New Zealand: Human Kinetics
Division of Sports Distributors NZ Ltd.
P.O. Box 300 226 Albany
North Shore City
Auckland
0064 9 448 1207
e-mail: info@humankinetics.co.nz

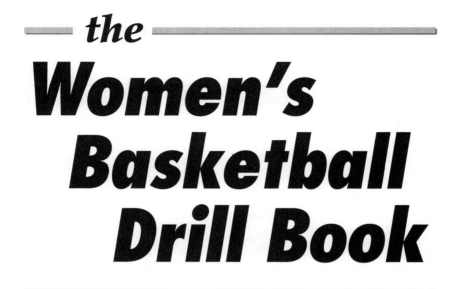

the
Women's
Basketball
Drill Book

Contents

Drill Finder

Drill Title	Page #	NUMBER OF PLAYERS		Primary Skills*	Off/Def/ Both	Fitness Building
		Small Group	Team			
CHAPTER 1: WARM-UP DRILLS						
Seven-on-Four	4		X		B	X
Circle Passing	6		X	P	B	X
Four Lines	8	X			D	X
Forty Seconds	10	X			O	X
Weave With Shots	12		X	D	D	X
Two-Ball Screen	14	X		Sc	D	X
Waves Passing	16		X	P	O	
Waves Sideline Passing	18		X	P	O	X
CHAPTER 2: CONDITIONING DRILLS						
Crazy 8	22	X		F, M	O	X
Zigzag	23		X	F, M	O	X
Speed Layups	24	X		P, Sh	O	X
Speed Scrimmage	25		X	M, Sh, T	B	X
Figure-8	26	X		P	O	X
The Box	28	X		F, R	B	X
Two-Line Long Passing and Layup	30	X		P, Sh	D	X
Thirty-Six Layups	32		X	R, Sh	O	X
Four Quarters	34	X		M	O	X
Stop, Score, Stop	35	X		Sh, T	D	X
Full-Court Layup	36		X	R, Sh	O	X
CHAPTER 3: MOVING DRILLS						
Three-Lane Movement	42	X		M, P	O	X
Three-Player Cutting	44	X		M, P, Sh	O	X
Tag	46	X		M	B	X
Wrap and Screen	48		X	M, P, Sh	B	X
Basket Cutting	50		X	M, P, Sh	B	X
X-Cutting	52		X	M, P	B	X
Argentinean Warm-Up	53	X		C, F, P	B	X
Maze Dribbling	54		X	D, F	B	X
Post Moves	55		X	D, F, M	B	X
Three Lines Full Court	56		X	C, M, P, Sh	B	X
CHAPTER 4: DRIBBLING DRILLS						
Snap and Touch	60		X	D	B	
Two-Ball High and Low	61		X	D	B	

*Primary Skills:
P for passing, C for catching, BH for ballhandling, M for moving, D for dribbling, Sc for screening, Sh for shooting, R for rebounding, T for transitioning, F for footwork.

(continued)

Drill Finder *(continued)*

Drill Title	Page #	NUMBER OF PLAYERS		Primary Skills*	Off/Def/ Both	Fitness Building
		Small Group	Team			
CHAPTER 6: OFFENSIVE SCREENING DRILLS (CONTINUED)						
Post Cross Screens: Flash High or Low	112	X		P, Sc	O	X
Off-Ball Screen	114	X		P, Sc, Sh	O	X
CHAPTER 7: SHOOTING DRILLS						
Olympic Shooting	118	X		P, R, Sh	O	X
Ticktock Shooting	119		X	Sh	O	
Shooting 100	120		X	P, Sh	O	
Three-Point Shooting	121	X		P, R, Sh	O	X
Fifty-Five-Second Shooting	122	X		F, Sh	O	
Zone Shooting	124	X		C, P, Sh	O	X
Thirty-Two	126	X		P, R, Sh	O	
Beat Lisa Leslie	127	X		P, R, Sh	O	
Rapid-Fire Shooting	128	X		P, R, Sh	O	
Transition Finishes	129		X	F, Sh, T	O	X
CHAPTER 8: OFFENSIVE REBOUNDING DRILLS						
Free Throw Rebounding	132	X		R	O	
Back Roll	133		X	R	O	
Five-on-Two Block-Out	134	X		M, R	O	X
Sixers Rebounding	136	X		M, P, R	O	X
Hit and Rebound	138	X		F, R	O	X
Two-Ball Rebounding	139	X		M, R	O	X
Two-on-Two, Weakside Rebounding	140	X		M, R	O	X
Figure-8 Rebounding	142	X		BH, R	O	X
Three-Line Rebounding	143	X		M, R, Sh	O	X
Three-on-Three, Three-on-Four	144	X		M, R, T	O	X
Competitive Rebounding	146		X	P, R, Sh	O	X
Circle Box-Out	147	X		R	O	X
Three-Player Weave, Weakside Box-Out	148	X		D, R, Sh	O	X
Box Out and Go	149	X		M, R	O	X
CHAPTER 9: OFFENSIVE TRANSITION DRILLS						
Break on Numbers	152	X		M, P, Sh, T	O	X
Celtics Fast Break	153		X	P, Sh	O	
Five-Lane Recognition	154	X		M, P, R	O	X
Three-on-Two, Two-on-One Continuous Conversion	156	X		M, P, Sh	O	X

*Primary Skills:
P for passing, C for catching, BH for ballhandling, M for moving, D for dribbling, Sc for screening, Sh for shooting, R for rebounding, T for transitioning, F for footwork.

(continued)

Drill Finder (continued)

Drill Title	Page #	NUMBER OF PLAYERS		Primary Skills*	Off/Def/ Both	Fitness Building
		Small Group	Team			
CHAPTER 12: DEFENSIVE REBOUNDING DRILLS						
Two-on-Two Rebounding	214	X		R	D	X
Sky and Fly	215		X	P, R	D	X
Game Time	216		X	R, Sh	D	X
Weakside Crashing	218	X		M, R	D	X
Winners and Losers	219	X		R, Sh	D	X
Triangle Box-Out	220	X		M, R	D	
Four-Player Shell Protection	221	X		M, R	D	X
Circle Box-Out	222	X		M, R	D	
Two-Player Defend and Rebound	224	X		P, R, Sh	D	
Ball in the Middle	225	X		M, R	D	X
O-D-O (Offense-Defense-Out)	226	X		P, R, Sh	D	
Rebound, Outlet Transition	228	X		M, R	D	X
Liberty Rebounding	230	X		M, R	D	X
Scramble Rebounding	232	X		M, R	D	X
Outlet Rebounding	234		X	P, R, Sh	D	X
CHAPTER 13: DEFENSIVE TRANSITION DRILLS						
Transition D: One-on-One	238	X		D	B	X
Catch-Up	239	X		M, T, F	D	X
Sideline Attack	240		X	M, Sc	D	X
Three-on-Three Defensive Transition	242		X	P, Sc	D	X
Three-on-Three-on-Three	244		X	M, Sh	B	X
VT Release	245	X		Sh, T	D	X
Olympic Defense	246	X		P, Sh, T	B	X
Two-on-Two Full: Defending On-Ball Screens	248		X	P, Sc, Sh	D	X
Two-on-Two Full: Basket Positioning	250	X		R, Sc, T	D	X
Full-Court Turn-and-Cut	252		X	Sc	D	X
Three-on-Two Plus One	253	X		T	D	X
Five-on-Four Plus One	254	X		Sh, T	D	X
Killer	256	X		BH, D, Sh	B	X
CHAPTER 14: TRANSITIONING DRILLS						
Doubling On-Ball Screens	260	X		F, Sc	B	X
On-Ball and Off-Ball Defense	262	X		M	D	
Help and Recover	264		X	M, P	B	

*Primary Skills:
P for passing, C for catching, BH for ballhandling, M for moving, D for dribbling, Sc for screening, Sh for shooting, R for rebounding, T for transitioning, F for footwork.

Drill Title	Page #	NUMBER OF PLAYERS		Primary Skills*	Off/Def/ Both	Fitness Building
		Small Group	Team			
Defensive Knockdown	265	X		M, R, Sc	D	X
Cutting Loose	266	X		M, Sc	D	X
Shell Defense	267	X		M, P	D	X
Timed Shell	268	X		D, M	D	X
One-on-One Force Corner	269	X		P, R	B	X
Wing Denial	270	X		Sc	D	X
Three-Player Help and Recover	271	X		P, T	B	X
Deny, Open, Deny	272	X		M, Sc	D	X
Deny the Ball, Take the Charge	273	X		M, Sc	D	X
Help and Recover to Three-on-Three Live	274	X		P, R	D	X
Defending Closeouts	276	X		P, T	B	X
CHAPTER 15: POST DRILLS						
Two-on-Two in the Post	280	X		M, Sc	B	X
One-on-One Post	281	X		C, M, P	B	X
Low-Post Pit	282	X		C, F, Sh	D	X
Post Defense	283	X		Sc	D	X
Post Denial	284	X		M, P	D	X
Five-Point Closeout	285		X	F, M	D	X
Two-on-Two Rebound With Closeout	286	X		M, P	D	X
Two-Ball Pickup	288	X		M	D	X
Four Passes	290	X		P	D	X
CHAPTER 16: TEAM DRILLS						
Three Screens (Four-on-Four)	294		X	Sc	B	X
Five-on-Four	295	X		M, P, Sh	B	X
Five-on-Five Shell	296	X		M	D	X
Three-on-Three Continuous Motion	298	X		M, Sc	D	X
Defending Cutters	300	X		F, M	D	X
Four Out Front (Transition Defense)	302		X	M, R	D	X
Three-on-Three Half-Court Defense	304	X		P, Sc	D	X
Post Defensive Drill With Help	306	X		M	D	X
Triangle Rebounding (Perimeter Series)	308	X		R	D	X
Triangle Rebounding (Post Series)	310	X		M, R	D	X

Foreword

We are very happy to present to you a collection of the finest drills for coaches to use during their practices to develop complete players and complete team. These drills are from the finest coaches of women's basketball in the country who are members of the Women's Basketball Coaches Association. Many of them have won regular season conference championships, conference tournament championships, and NCAA championships. These drills are described in such a manner that less experienced coaches and players can understand and implement them, yet they promote the fundamental techniques needed to succeed at even the highest levels of play. Honing skills by constant use of specifically designed drills will insure improved performance of any player.

We would like to thank the 53 college coaches who contributed, without compensation, the drills that are used for this book. The proceeds of this book will help fund the Betty F. Jaynes Internship Program at the WBCA. Many young men and women who have participated in this program have gone on to become college athletic administrators, conference office administrators, director of basketball operations, event planners, corporate marketers, and of course, coaches.

One of the missions of the WBCA is to provide to coaches with instructional resources that will contribute to their team's success. We encourage you to refer to this drill book and use it often.

Beth Bass, CEO of the Women's Basketball Coaches Association
Betty Jaynes, Consultant of the Women's Basketball Coaches Association

Preface

Missing a layup. Not using a screen well. Turning it over with the game on the line. These offensive mistakes often are the difference between winning and losing. And we all know the old saying "Offense sells tickets, but defense wins games." Basketball players and teams who are consistently successful know this coaching cliché to be true.

To minimize costly mistakes on both ends of the court, players must have the ability to execute the game's basic skills day in and day out. The key to developing these fundamentals lies in repetition, and this book is packed with drills that teach players to execute like champions and keep practices from becoming stale. Almost 200 of the finest drills from the top coaches in today's game are divided into three categories—training, offense, and defense—and develop every aspect of the game.

Part I contains 19 training and conditioning drills. The drills in chapter 1 help players warm up and get ready for the rigors and movements of a practice or game. Chapter 2 focuses on developing the basketball-specific endurance and stamina players need to play at their best all game long.

The 83 drills in part II improve all aspects of a player's offensive game. Players will hone their ability to cut, slash, pivot, explode, and stop on a dime with the drills in chapter 3. Chapter 4 provides outstanding ballhandling drills for all five players on the floor. The drills in chapter 5 develop not only a player's understanding of when and where to deliver a pass so that it leads to a scoring opportunity, but also the physical ability to throw and catch the pass. Chapter 6 breaks down the art of setting and using screening to perfect an uncanny knack for getting open. The shooting drills in chapter 7, then, ensure that players have the tools to finish the job. Not every shot goes in, of course, so the drills in chapter 8 provide practice for the positioning and hustle needed to get second-chance opportunities. Rebounds often lead to fast breaks, and the drills in chapter 9 show how to put up points in transition.

Finally, part III provides 84 drills to enhance play on the defensive end. The footwork drills in chapter 10 are the first step to sound positioning and movement fundamentals. In chapter 11, screening drills help players disrupt the opposition's attempts to run two-player sets and offensive patterns. Frequent and intense work on the rebounding drills in chapter 12 will improve performance on the boards. The defensive transitioning drills in chapter 13 teach players to get back and stop the ball, turning the tables on the offense by eliminating their preferred options and opportunities for quick scoring. Chapters 14 and 15 provide drills that work on and polish a player's defensive perimeter and post skills. The final chapter in the book presents drills to put the team stamp on your defensive approach, coordinating the individual players on defensive units and helping them become a singular force instead of five separate pieces.

Champions reliably execute the fundamentals of the game. This book offers you a special collection of practice drills and coaching points from champion coaches to develop and hone individual and team performance on both ends of the court. Being sound fundamentally doesn't increase your chances of making the TV highlights, but it does make it much more likely that you'll cut down the nets at the end of the season. By incorporating these drills into your practices today, you just might be able to hang banners tomorrow.

Key to Diagrams

O	Offensive player
X	Defensive player
Ⓒ	Coach
M	Manager
Ⓟ	Passer
R	Rebounder
Ⓧ	Perimeter player
P	Post
G	Guard
W	Wing
⊕	Ball
⟶	Movement without the ball
- - - ➤	Pass or shot
—————⊣	Screen
—————(	Block out
——⁄—➤	Block pass
∿∿∿➤	Dribble

Training and Conditioning

chapter 1

Warm-Up Drills

Warming up for practices and games is critical to the success and safety of each individual's and the team's collective performance. Warm-up drills prepare the athletes' bodies for the overall rigorous effort that is about to be required and for the specific skills that will be used during competition or practice.

When appropriate drills are performed correctly, athletes will begin to enter a prepared state physically that will keep them from being injured, and mentally that will narrow their focus for the upcoming workout or competition. If the drills are not performed correctly or at the proper intensity, the chances of the athlete becoming injured will increase. This applies to every level of player. Even, and perhaps especially, at the pro level, players take the warm-up for both practice and games very seriously. Make sure every athlete is ready to play by successfully warming up with these drills.

SEVEN-ON-FOUR

Carey Green | *Liberty University*

Purpose

To work on defensive fundamentals and defensive rotation on a drive from the baseline and on getting through off-ball screens.

Organization

An offensive player stands at each corner of the lane with a defender on each player. Two coaches (or offensive players) are on the baseline, and one is at the top of the key with the ball.

Procedure

1. The ball starts at the top, and each defender guards her player (see figure 1).
2. The coach at the top says "go," and the offensive players at the elbows screen down for those at the blocks. The offensive players at the blocks replace the players positioned at the elbows. The defenders play according to the coach's philosophy for the type of screen implemented. The coach says "go" again, and another down screen takes place.
3. The coach can pass to either of the coaches at the baseline.
4. When that coach says "go," the offensive players on the elbow and block closest to the coach screen away. The opposite offensive players replace these players on the block and elbow according to the team's philosophy on screens (see figure 2).
5. The coach skips the ball to the opposite coach on the baseline and the same kind of screen occurs.
6. Whenever the coach on the baseline has the ball, she or he can drive the baseline and try to score. The defenders need to react and rotate to help (again, established earlier by the coach's philosophy).
7. The ball continues to skip around the top, until a coach sees an opening to pass to an offensive player or decides to drive and score.

Coaching Points

- Emphasize proper defensive techniques, such as jumping to the ball, opening up to let a teammate through, and sitting on a screen.
- Emphasize communication on defense.
- On offense, stress waiting for screens and using screens.

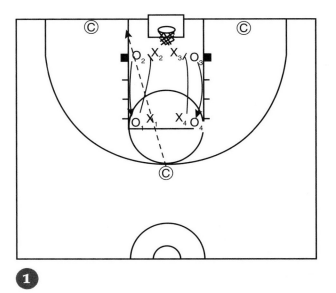

1

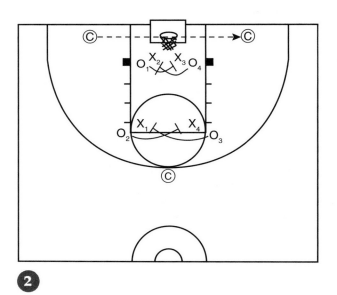

2

2   CIRCLE PASSING

Carey Green | *Liberty University*

Purpose

To develop the ability to concentrate and communicate during chaos and to execute proper passing form and footwork.

Organization

Use at least nine people for the drill. Six (or more) stand in a circle; three of them hold balls. Three people stand in the middle of the circle facing the six. The circle should be big enough for comfortable chest or bounce passes between the middle and the outside of the circle.

Procedure

1. Players with the balls make a chest pass to the person they face in the middle of the circle.
2. The player who just passed follows her pass to midcircle, jump-stops, and reverse pivots in the direction of the flow of traffic (before the drill starts, the coach decides whether players go clockwise or counterclockwise). If going clockwise, the passer jump-stops and reverse pivots to the left. After the reverse pivot, the player has her hands ready to catch a pass.
3. After receiving the pass, the player who started in the middle of the circle passes to the person on the right of where the ball came from (if going clockwise).
4. This same player immediately follows her pass, jump stops at the location, and reverse pivots to the right (if going clockwise) with hands ready to receive another pass.
5. This motion continues until the coach stops the drill or makes a variation.

Coaching Points

- Emphasize proper passing form and catching form: hands always ready for the pass.
- Emphasize the jump stop and reverse pivots.
- Demand that players communicate at all times, whether it's saying names or using basketball chatter.

Variations

- Change from chest pass to bounce pass.
- Change from clockwise to counterclockwise.
- Alternate a chest pass and a bounce pass on subsequent passes.

FOUR LINES

Christina Wielgus | *Dartmouth College*

Purpose

To incorporate offensive skills relevant to the motion offense. To rehearse ball reversal and of the motion offense while warming up.

Organization

Divide the team evenly into four lines: to the side of the basket and each player with a ball, a line off each elbow, and one at the top of the key.

Procedure

1. The player under the basket (O_1) passes the ball out from under the basket to the person at the closest elbow (O_2). Player O_1 follows her pass and goes to the end of the receiving line.
2. Player O_2 times her movement to meet the ball. She catches the ball, sweeps it to the floor, and passes it to the player at the top of the key (O_3). She follows her pass to the end of that line.
3. Player O_3 sweeps the ball low and passes it to the remaining wing (O_4). She follows her pass to the end of that line.
4. Player O_4 takes a shot. The coach can determine the type of shot. The shooter gets her own rebound, keeps the ball, and goes to the end of the line under the basket.
5. As the shot is being taken, the next person in the line under the basket starts the ball reversal.

Coaching Points

- This drill gets the players moving quickly.
- Players should time the pop to receive the ball.
- Players should sweep the ball to the floor so that they can see the post.

Variation

Add any element of your offense to the ball reversal by calling out the option. For example, the last two players receiving the ball form an on-ball screen. The first time through the drill use the screen. The next time hit the roller. The next time, the person with the ball goes opposite the screen.

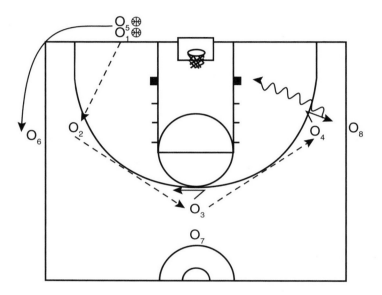

FORTY SECONDS

Christina Wielgus | *Dartmouth College*

Purpose

To get the players moving full court in a manner relevant to the team's offense.

Organization

Use five players that are positionally correct. Each player takes a predetermined shot in a prescribed order.

Procedure

1. The coach tosses the ball off the glass. A fast break is run, with O_5 outletting the ball to the wing (O_1), who passes it ahead to O_2. Player O_2 attempts a three-point shot. If she misses, players rebound it and put it in (see figure 1).
2. If the shot is made, O_5 takes it out of bounds, and players run the fast break in the other direction. The first post down (O_4) takes the next shot from the block. If she misses, players rebound it and put it in (see figure 2).
3. If the shot is made, O_5 takes it out of bounds, and players run the fast break in the other direction. Player O_2 makes a skip pass to O_3, who is on the weak side, for a three-pointer. If she misses, players rebound it and put it in (see figure 3).
4. If the shot is made, O_5 takes it out of bounds, and players run the fast break in the other direction. The trailing forward (O_5) takes the next shot at the top of the key. If she misses, the rebound is put in (see figure 4).
5. If the shot is made, O_5 takes it out of bounds, and players run the fast break in the other direction. For the last shot, O_1 dribbles the length of the court for a layup. If she misses, the rebound is put in (see figure 5).
6. A missed rebound must be put in before the drill continues.
7. The group has 40 seconds to complete the drill. If they don't, they repeat it.

Coaching Points

- Communication is important as the players take the shot assigned to them.
- Players must hustle to complete the drill in 40 seconds.
- Turnovers, missed shots, and lack of hustle will take care of themselves as the players attempt to complete the drill.

Variation

Vary the sequence and types of shots. For example, the last guard assigned a layup must use a screen set by a forward.

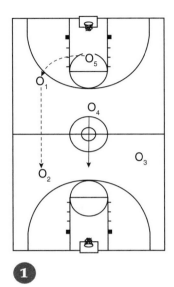

1

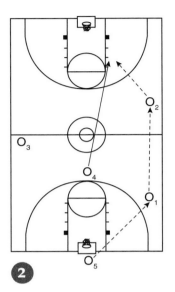

2

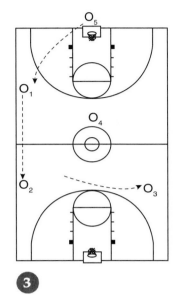

3

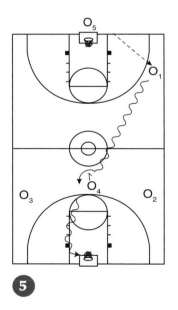

4

5

5   WEAVE WITH SHOTS

Christina Wielgus | *Dartmouth College*

Purpose

To get the players passing and moving quickly so they can take lots of shots.

Organization

Players form three lines under the basket. The second players in each of the outside lines have a ball. The first player in the middle line has a ball. Two coaches, each with a ball, stand to the right and left of the other basket.

Procedure

1. On the coach's command, the player in the middle line passes to a wing. She cuts behind the person she just passed to. The line continues to weave down the court. The player closest to the basket (O_1) takes a layup, grabs the rebound, and steps out of bounds (see figure 1).
2. The two wing players (O_2 and O_3) spot up for an outside shot each. The coaches pass each of them a ball, and they shoot.
3. Player O_1 inbounds the layup ball. She passes to O_3, who has just popped to the wing. The line weaves back down the court (see figure 2).
4. The person closest to the basket takes a layup. The two other weaving players receive a pass from the next wings in line, who each have a ball.
5. The person waiting in the middle line grabs the ball after the layup is made and passes it to the waiting wings who have just passed the ball to the spot shooters.
6. The weaving process begins again with one layup and two jump shots taken at each end.

Coaching Points

- Make sure the players do not travel.
- Emphasize the concept of passing and moving and gathering before taking a shot.
- Remind players to make sharp and crisp passes.
- Encourage players to talk about where they are on the floor in relation to the ball. The passer should call out the receiver's name.

Variation

If space is limited, use half of the court.

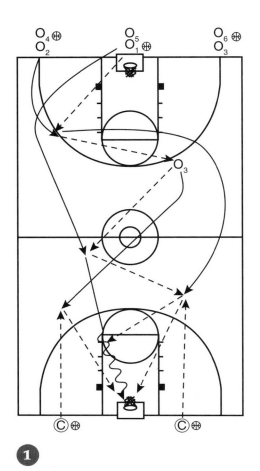

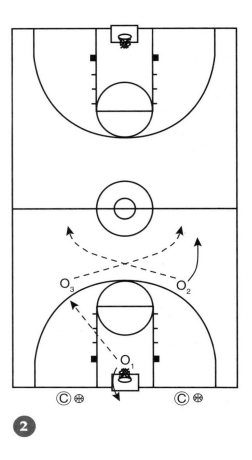

TWO-BALL SCREEN

Christina Wielgus | *Dartmouth College*

Purpose

To take warm-up shots that are relevant to the team's offense.

Organization

Players form two lines: one at half-court, the other in the wing. Two coaches are in the other wing; the one closest to the baseline starts with a ball and can have extras on the ground in case one gets away from a player. The first couple of players in line at half-court have balls.

Procedure

1. Player O_1, at the point with the ball, passes to C_1. She then goes and sets a screen for the wing player (O_2) (see figure 1).
2. The wing player uses the screen and comes straight toward C_1 to receive a pass. She shoots.
3. Meanwhile, O_1 has shaped to the ball. She receives a pass from C_2 and shoots (see figure 2).
4. Shooters rebound their own shots, then go around the outside of the drill and pass the ball back to the ball's original line.

Coaching Points

- Emphasize all aspects of setting and using screens.
- Remind players to talk through the screening action. For example, the player being screened should say "straight" or "curl," depending on how she is using the screen.
- Teach players to follow their shots.

Variation

Use this format for all screening options: How the screen is used and who goes high and who goes low determines the location of the pass to the shooter.

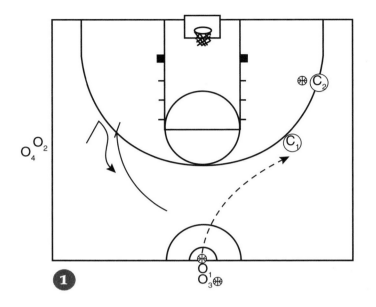

1

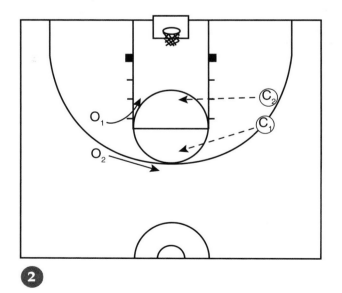

2

WAVES PASSING

Julie Rousseau | *Pepperdine University*

Purpose

To work on passing and sharp cutting and to emphasize communication, rebounding, and the outlet pass.

Organization

Two lines of players are at half-court. One line shoots layups, and the other line executes a rebound and outlet. Two players stationed near the free throw line face each other: one at the elbow and the other near the sideline at the free throw line extended. On the opposite sideline at the free throw line extended, two players form the outlet line. Use two balls.

Procedure

1. Players O_1 and O_5 each have a ball.
2. To start the drill, O_1 passes to O_3 and at the same time, O_5 passes to O_7.
3. Player O_1 cuts for a layup, and O_5 follows her pass to the end of the rebound line at half-court
4. Player O_3 passes to O_4, while O_1 sprints to the basket for a layup.
5. Player O_1 receives a pass from O_4 and shoots a layup.
6. Player O_3 follows behind O_1 by sprinting over the top of the elbow and rebounds the ball (see figure 1).
7. Player O_3 outlets to O_6 and follows the pass to the end of outlet line. Player O_1 returns immediately to replace O_4 at the elbow (see figure 2).
8. After the pass to O_1, O_4 sprints to replace O_3 on sideline.
9. After O_5 passes to O_7, O_7 passes across the court to O_2.
10. All passers follow their pass to the next designated line.

Coaching Points

- The players and the ball must move quickly from one position to the next.
- Players must communicate.
- Cuts must be sharp and precise.
- The ball should not hit the floor after the layup is made.

Variations

- Have beginners execute the drill with one ball.
- Set a target time for the drill; for example, make 15 layups in one minute.
- Have players shoot both right- and left-handed layups.
- Allow creative passing for fun, for example, between the legs, behind the back, and over the shoulder.

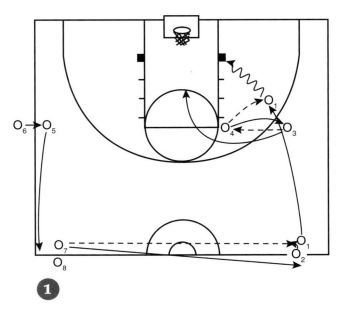

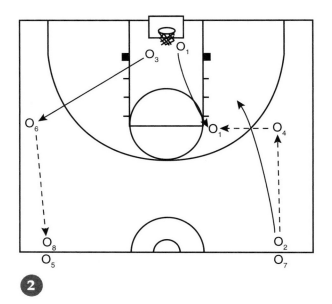

WAVES SIDELINE PASSING

Julie Rousseau | *Pepperdine University*

Purpose

To develop conditioning by emphasizing the player movements, passing, and communication used during a fast break.

Organization

The drill requires two balls. Most of the players line up out of bounds on the baseline. Three other spots along the sideline and a spot on the end line are occupied during the drill.

Procedure

1. The first two players in the line have balls. Player O_1 starts the drill by inbounding the ball to O_2. At this point, O_5 starts sprinting down the floor opposite the ball. Player O_2 catches the pass, pivots, and passes the ball to O_3. Player O_3 receives the ball and passes to O_4. As soon as O_4 catches the ball, O_5, who has been sprinting, makes a diagonal cut at the elbow opposite the ball, receives the pass from O_4, and shoots a layup on the ballside block.
2. At the start of the drill, after O_1 inbounds the ball to O_2, she sprints down the middle of the court and rebounds the ball that O_5 shoots for a layup.
3. After O_1 rebounds the ball, she takes the ball out of bounds (without allowing the ball to hit the floor) on the opposite baseline and inbounds to O_2, and the drill repeats going toward the other end.
4. After each player has performed the drill on both sides of the court, players rotate to fill the next vacant spot on the floor. Player O_1 rotates to O_2's original spot near the free throw line, O_2 rotates to O_3's original spot at half-court, O_3 rotates to O_4's original spot near the other free throw line, O_4 rotates into O_5's original spot on the opposite lane line, and O_5 becomes the shooter.
5. The second player in the line (O_6) inbounds the ball to the original O_1.
6. The drill continues until all players have completed the rotation twice, shooting two right-handed and two left-handed layups.

Coaching Points

- With all players running to negotiate their next spot, communication is imperative for the success of the drill.
- All players must meet the pass with a jump stop, pivot facing the court, and step toward the next player.
- The ball should not hit the floor after an attempted layup.

Variations

- Set a goal and designate a time limit, for example, challenge the team to make 10 layups in one minute.
- Change the types of passes used in the drill from chest to bounce or overhead pass.

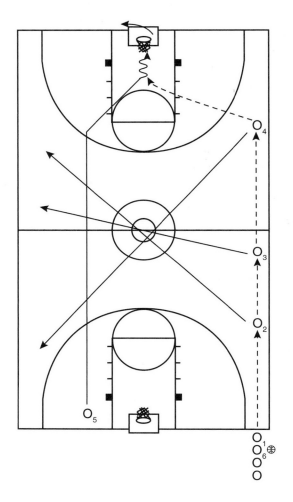

chapter 2

Conditioning Drills

As coaches always tell their team, it's the work players do in the off-season that sets the stage for the season's sucess, and conditioning is a huge part of that effort. As players prepare for the season, conditioning drills are a reminder of what needs to be done to get the athlete ready for the season. It is a program involving drills that daily and progressively prepare the basketball player for the battle of the teams during the season. Teams that are not in condition, no matter what type of athletes they are, will fail in the end when the pressure is on to make a free throw, field goal, three point shot, or steal. An athlete who knows her body is ready for the season is an athlete who is going to be successful and play with more confidence. Conditioning is the foundation for the success of the season. These drills give the coach a reference that will take conditioning to another level. Use these resources and see your team advance.

CRAZY 8

Brian Giorgis | *Marist College*

Purpose

To condition players by using different defensive slides and to promote communication.

Organization

Coaches and managers are on each end line and sideline. The head coach is at half-court. Players line up at one corner of the court.

Procedure

1. The first player slides up the sideline to midcourt, alternating the lead foot every two slides. She then slides across midcourt and follows a figure-8 pattern to the end of the line.
2. The next player starts when the player in front of her reaches midcourt.
3. All players yell "ball, ball, ball," throughout the slide.
4. Once the Crazy 8 lap is completed, the player gets in line and starts again when the player in front of her reaches midcourt.
5. Players always face the same direction throughout the slide.

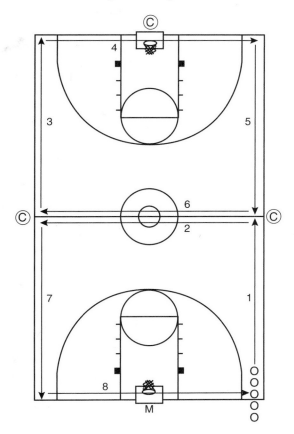

Coaching Points

- Make sure that players stay in the desired positions throughout the slide and that they continue communicating.
- Teach players proper technique as they slide forward and slide using a drop step.

Variations

- Add sprints or backpedals to certain areas of the 8.
- Designate the length of the drill by time or number of 8s to complete.

10   ZIGZAG

Brian Giorgis | Marist College

Purpose

To improve ballhandling under pressure, one-on-one defensive skills, and conditioning.

Organization

The head coach is in the middle of the floor. Pairs of players, an offensive and defensive player, form two lines on opposite corners of the court.

Procedure

1. The offensive player starts on the end line between the sideline and foul lane, with the defender tight.
2. The offensive player dribbles at a 45-degree angle toward foul line. The defender plays good, tight, player-to-player defense.
3. At the foul line, the defender "jumps the ball" to force the offensive player in the opposite direction.
4. The offensive player uses a change-of-direction dribble to go 45 degrees toward the sideline.
5. Each player zigzags down court until she gets to the coach at the opposite end.
6. Once she reaches other end, the coach says "go," and the offensive player goes one-on-one to basket.
7. After the shot, both players go to the opposite line and switch positions (offense to defense, defense to offense).

Coaching Points

- The offensive player should use all four change-of-direction dribbles: crossover, spin, between the legs, and behind the back.
- The offensive player should shield the ball from the defender and use a proper dribbling stance.
- The change of direction should be quick and sharp.
- The defensive player needs to be in a proper on-the-ball defensive stance and use a proper sliding technique.
- All zigzags should simulate movements made in a game.

Variation

Focus on just one or two types of change-of-direction dribbles.

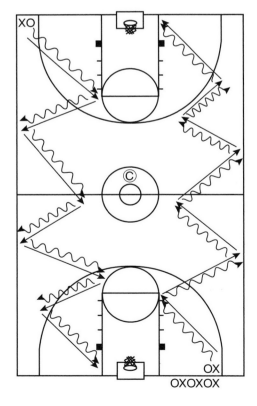

11   SPEED LAYUPS

Brian Giorgis | *Marist College*

Purpose

To practice layups and power slides at full speed on both sides of the floor while improving conditioning and stamina.

Organization

Four coaches or managers stand at designated spots on the floor. Players split in two groups and line up at opposite corners of the court.

Procedure

1. The first player in line passes the ball to the coach at the foul line and then sprints down the court.
2. The coach passes the ball back to the player, who then passes to the coach at the opposite foul line. The player may take one or two dribbles before passing the ball. The player sprints to receive the pass back from coach.
3. The coach on the opposite foul line passes back to the player, who then goes full speed for a layup.

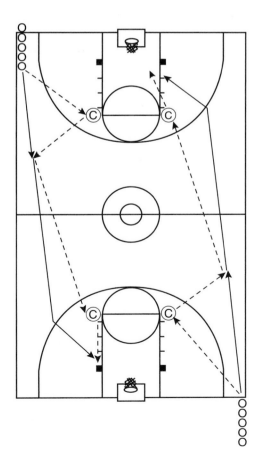

4. The player rebounds her own shot and goes to end of the line at that end of the court.
5. The next player in line starts after the first coach passes back to the player who previously started the drill.
6. One side always shoots a layup (off the proper foot); the other side does a power slide off two feet.

Coaching Points

- Demand that players go full speed and remain under control.
- Make sure players use proper footwork for the layup and power slide.

Variations

- Have players perform layups for a certain amount of time and power slides for a certain amount of time.
- Make the drill competitive by challenging players to make a certain number of shots in a set amount of time.
- Players, instead of coaches and managers, can be passers. If so, rotate passers after every minute.

12 SPEED SCRIMMAGE

Brian Giorgis | Marist College

Purpose

To improve conditioning by creating gamelike conditions without dead-ball situations and forcing continuous transition, both offensively and defensively.

Organization

Use five offensive and five defensive players. Each coach stands at the sidelines with a ball, and a manager is the chaser who goes after errant balls and gives them to any coach without a ball.

Procedure

1. Players play five on five, full court, with the following restrictions.
2. On change of possession, all players must cross half-court within three seconds.
3. The shot clock is reduced to 18 seconds.
4. Substitutions are made on the fly and only for a player who has been on the court for at least two minutes.
5. No free throws are taken.
6. Balls that go out of bounds are immediately put back in play by the nearest coach, who passes it to any player.
7. Players fouled in the act of shooting are given points and the ball is put back in play immediately to the opposing team.
8. If coaches need to give a player instructions, substitutions are made on the fly, and instruction is given.
9. Consequences for not meeting restrictions (for example, not making it to midcourt within three seconds) are assigned at the end of the drill or scrimmage.

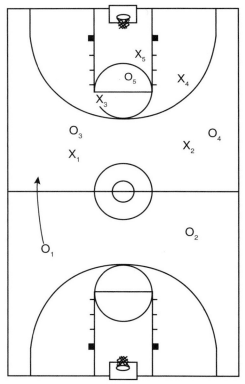

Coaching Points

- Emphasize the transition defense and the communication necessary for its success.
- Stress proper execution of your transition offense and motion principles.
- Emphasize maintaining focus and properly executing when fatigued.

Variations

- Play five on five on five, or four on four on four, or three on three on three without subs.
- Make the drill competitive by keeping score.

FIGURE-8

Leslie Crane | *Western Illinois University*

Purpose

To condition players while working on full-court passing, concentrating, and communicating between team members.

Organization

Players form three lines: two outside passing lines on either side of the court at the three-point line and a middle line on one side of the lane. Each person in the middle line has a ball.

Procedure

1. Player O_2 passes the ball to the closest team member, O_3, and follows her pass by running behind O_3. At the same time, O_1 runs up the court to the ball to receive a short pass from O_3.
2. After O_3 passes to O_1, she follows her pass and cuts behind O_1. At the same time, O_2 has cut up the floor to the ball to receive a pass from O_1.
3. After O_1 passes to O_2, she follows her pass and cuts behind O_2, while O_3 runs up the floor to the ball for a short pass from O_2. This procedure continues down the floor until all three players reach the opposite end.
4. To add a layup, O_3 passes to O_1 for the layup; then O_3 runs behind O_1 and touches the baseline. Player O_1 shoots the layup and runs to touch the baseline opposite O_3, and O_2 rebounds the ball before it hits the floor.

Coaching Points

- Players should run to the ball in order to shorten the passes, which will prevent rainbow passes and traveling violations.
- Players should show a target hand to pass to, and their hands should be up at all times to catch and pass the ball.
- Players must call for the ball.
- Players should shoot a true layup off the glass, not execute a finger roll.

Variations

- When starting out, use weighted balls to help build strength in player's passing. The heavier ball also make players run to the ball and shorten the pass.
- Designate the number of passes players must make before shooting a layup. Five is a good number to start with. Also designate the number of layups they must make before changing players.
- As the players' conditioning improves, lower the number of passes and increase the number of layups to help players learn to make layups whether there is a defense or not. Because they cannot come out of the drill until they make a certain number of layups, they will concentrate on making them.
- Consider a dropped ball of any kind a turnover, and stop the drill and have the entire team run a sprint. This will help increase concentration during passing and receiving the ball.

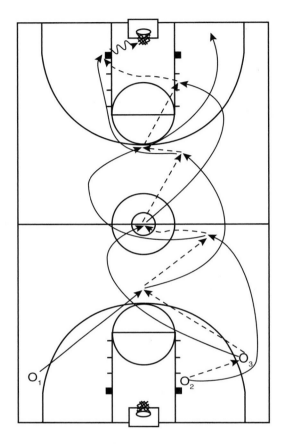

14   THE BOX

Leslie Crane | *Western Illinois University*

Purpose

To improve conditioning and footwork and to practice changing shooting focus. This drill simulates game conditions by requiring players to sprint to the basket to rebound and to backpedal for defense and to change their focus while shooting.

Organization

Use two basketballs and four players: two passers, who have the balls; a shooter stationed above block; and a long rebounder.

Procedure

1. Passer 1 passes the ball to the shooter, (O_1), who turns and shoots a drop-step shot then proceeds to the opposite block. Passer 1 follows her pass and runs in and rebounds the ball before it hits the floor (see figure 1). After rebounding, passer 1 backpedals to her passing position at the three-point line and the free throw line extended.
2. Passer 2 passes to the shooter as she comes across the lane for another block shot. She follows her pass and runs into the lane to rebound the ball and then backpedals to her position at the three-point line and free throw line extended (see figure 2).
3. The shooter continues alternating shots from each block until she hears the whistle for a change. When that occurs the shooter stays on one side of the lane and shoots block shots and elbow or T-shots. The shooter backpedals up to the elbow after shooting at the block and dives hard to the block after shooting at the elbow. Passer 2 comes in to rebound and passes to passer 1, who is a stationary passer now (see figure 3). The rebounder at the top of the key assists with long rebounds only. The shooter continues alternating shots from the elbow and block until she hears the whistle to change.
4. Now the shooter alternates shots from both elbows. The passers become active and pass in and rebound the ball then backpedal to their passing positions as they did before. The rebounder at the top of the key rebounds long rebounds only (see figure 4).
5. The shooter continues to alternate elbow shots until she hears the whistle to change. At that time, the shooter alternates shots from the elbow and block on the opposite side of the lane from where she began. The passers become stationary as they were before, except that now passer 1 comes in to rebound and passes out to passer 2. The rebounder at the top of the key gathers the long rebounds (see figure 5).
6. The shooter continues until the whistle sounds. When that occurs, the shooter returns to shoot alternating block shots, and the passers become active again, rebounding the ball before it hits the floor and backpedaling to their passing positions (see figure 6).

Coaching Points

- Remind shooters to keep one or both hands up as a target for the passers.
- Tell passers what type of passes to use.
- Have passers sprint in to rebound and backpedal to their starting positions. This will improve conditioning and footwork.
- Tell shooters where their focus should be for each shot: for example, for block shots use the glass, and focus on the corner of the square on the backboard; for elbow shots, look into the middle of the cylinder.

Variations

- Vary the duration of the drill. Start with 20 seconds for each type of shot and increase the time as the players' conditioning improves.
- Insert a coach with a blocking pad to initiate contact when the player shoots block shots and to put a hand up to distract the player when she is attempting elbow shots.
- Rotate players: passer 1 to long rebounder to passer 2 to shooter. A new person steps into the passer 1 position.

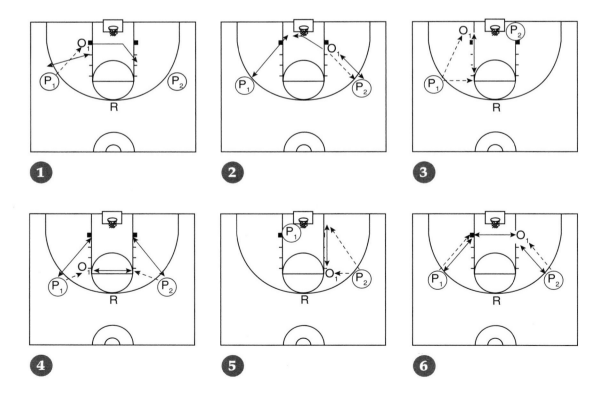

15 TWO-LINE LONG PASSING AND LAYUP

Leslie Crane | *Western Illinois University*

Purpose

To improve conditioning and develop concentration during fast-break passing and while shooting full-speed layups.

Organization

Use 4 to 16 players and four basketballs. Divide players into four lines, two on each end of the court.

Procedure

1. On the whistle, the first player in line O_1 dribbles twice to reach the half-court line.
2. At the same time, the first player in line O_2 sprints to the basket on the opposite end.
3. Player O_1 passes the ball to player O_2, who catches it and shoots a layup (see figure 1).
4. When player O_1 reaches the half-court line, player O_3 makes two dribbles to the half-court and player O_4 sprints to the basket on the opposite end (see figure 2).
5. When players O_3 and O_4 reach half-court, the next players in line behind O_1 and O_2 start their entrance into the drill.

Coaching Points

- The shooter must have a target hand up for the passer.
- The dribbler/passer must have control of the ball and push it out in front to cover more court area.
- The shooter must call out the passer's name.
- The shooter cannot dribble before shooting, and the shooter and passer must time their sprint and pass for a layup.

Variations

- Add a coach for defense against the shooter or passer.
- Designate a number of layups to be made in a certain amount of time, for example, 65 layups in two minutes.

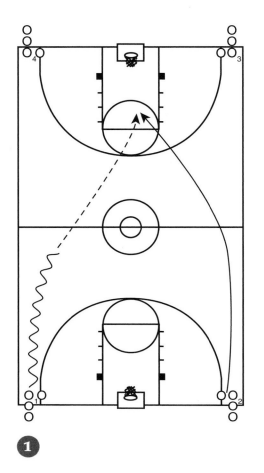

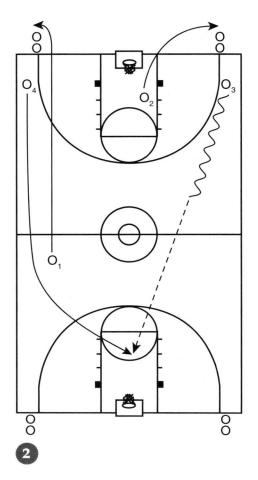

1

2

THIRTY-SIX LAYUPS

Ed Swanson | *Sacred Heart University*

Purpose

To improve conditioning and develop the ability to finish while tired.

Organization

Break the team into groups of three. The first group starts on the sideline at half-court, all facing one direction. The rest of the groups line up behind them. Use two balls.

Procedure

1. Player O_1 dribbles in for a layup.
2. Player O_2 goes in for the rebound (see figure 1).
3. Player O_3, the trailer, runs up and touches the three-point line, and then heads out wide down the court toward the opposite basket the other way.
4. Player O_2 makes an outlet pass to O_1, who then leads O_3 with a pass for a layup.
5. After O_2 outlets the ball to O_1, she becomes the trailer. She runs down and touches the three-point line and then returns back up the court (see figure 2).
6. Continue until the group has made nine layups.
7. As soon as the first group of three makes nine, the second group begins. If a layup is missed, the whole team starts over. Continue until the team makes 36 layups in a row.

Coaching Points

- Players should talk to each other when they are tired.
- Players should make good outlet passes and lead the shooter into her layup.

Variation

Make the drill competitive by challenging each group to make as many layups as they can in two minutes.

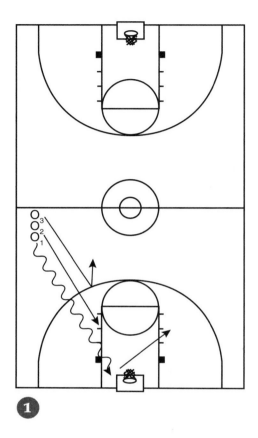

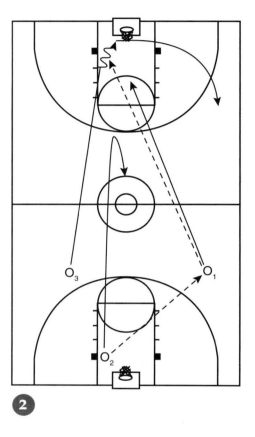

17   FOUR QUARTERS

Ed Swanson | *Sacred Heart University*

Purpose

To improve conditioning.

Organization

Split the team into two groups on the baseline. One group completes one quarter of the drill, and then the other group goes.

Procedure

1. Group 1 runs four sprints (down the court and back is one). When they are done, group 2 runs the sprints.
2. Group 1 runs four suicides. Group 1 rests while group 2 is running.
3. Group 1 sprints to half-court and then backpedals to the other baseline four times (down and back is one). Group 2 repeats the same actions.
4. Group 1 does defensive slides to half-court and then sprints to the opposite baseline four times (down and back is one). Then group 2 goes.

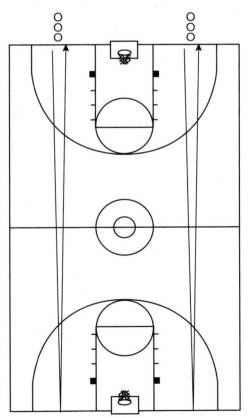

Coaching Points

- Everybody must sprint all out. Players should not save anything for later.
- Teammates should encourage each other, each group cheering on the other.
- The group resting must stand upright, no bending over or hands on the knees.

Variation

Establish time limits for each quarter to make it more urgent.

18 STOP, SCORE, STOP

Ed Swanson | Sacred Heart University

Purpose

To improve conditioning while working on half-court and transition offense and defense.

Organization

Two teams of five players play a game to three points.

Procedure

1. The offensive team starts with the ball at half-court, and the two teams play live.
2. If the offense scores, they get a point and the ball back on top.
3. If the defense steals or gets a rebound, they play it live and try to score on the opposite end.
4. If the defensive team scores, they have to get back and get another stop before they get the point.
5. If the defensive team gets its initial stop and then doesn't score, the offensive team gets the ball back at the top of the key and tries to score again.
6. Play at least twice so that each team has a turn at playing offense and defense.
7. The losing team runs a suicide in between games.

Coaching Points

- The odds are stacked against the defensive team. It is much more difficult for them to get a point.
- Challenge the defensive team to win, while also challenging the offense to take advantage of their position.
- Intensity and playing to win are the keys.

Variation

Instead of playing to three points, play for a certain amount of time, for example, five minutes, then switch offense and defensive teams and play five more minutes. At the end of the two segments, see who has the most points. The losing team runs.

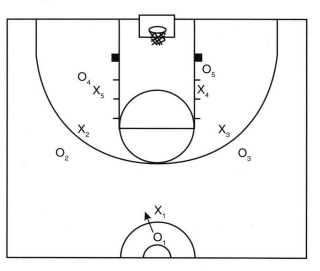

FULL-COURT LAYUP

Ed Swanson | *Sacred Heart University*

Purpose

To get everyone to work together and stay focused while improving conditioning.

Organization

Four lines of players start at half-court: A line of shooters and rebounders face each basket. Each line of shooters has a ball. Two coaches stand at half-court next to the rebounding lines. Three minutes are on the clock.

Procedure

1. When the clock starts, the players with the balls dribble in from half-court to take a layup (see figure 1).
2. A player from each rebounding line grabs the ball and flips it to the next player heading in from half-court.
3. The rebounder runs full court to the shooting line at the opposite basket.
4. The shooter touches the coach's hand on her side of half-court, and joins the rebounding line on that side of the court (see figure 2).
5. If a player misses or drops a ball, the drill is done again until it is completed with no errors.

Coaching Points

- Because running the lanes can get hectic with the rebounder flipping the ball to the next shooter and then running full court while the rebounder on the other side is doing the same thing, players must communicate with each other.
- Players must move at full speed.
- Because this drill simulates game speed, it teaches players to be accurate and controlled in a high-stress, full-speed, and sometimes chaotic environment.

Variation

Instead of punishing for misses, give the team a goal and count the layups made.

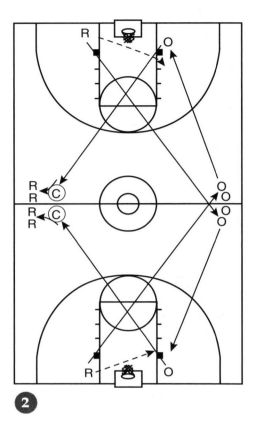

Offensive Skills

chapter 3

Moving Drills

Watch any outstanding basketball player and you will notice two common traits: great body balance and control. Tamika Catchings, Siemone Augustus, and Chamique Holdsclaw all exemplify the world-class athlete who balances great speed and agility with strength and quickness. Simply put, they are hard to stop.

A successful player in today's game must have tremendous footwork—either natural or learned—and the ability to cut, slash, pivot, explode, and stop abruptly. Developing sound footwork within the context of game situations and live play is a challenge for any coach. And although most athletes do not relish foot-fire, pivoting, and stopping drills, these are the fundamentals that must be mastered to excel in competition in the fast-paced style of today's women's game.

The drills presented in the following section will help you shape your players' enthusiasm for the game and provide them with a framework to develop other skills. Review them often and drill them daily, and your players will react and perform under pressure with amazing grace.

Pat Summitt | *University of Tennessee*

Purpose

To help develop skill in moving without the ball.

Organization

Use three offensive players.

Procedure

1. Players start on the baseline: one on the right side, one in the middle, and one on the left side of the court.
2. The ball starts in the middle (see figure 1).
3. The outside players cut and then come back to the ball.
4. The player in the middle passes the ball to one side to begin the drill; no dribbling at first.
5. The other two players cut and come back to the ball until they reach the other end of the court.

Coaching Points

- Players must stay in their lane.
- Timing is important. Players must time their cuts and get open when the passer is ready to deliver the pass.

Variations

- Add defensive players (see figure 2).
- Allow two dribbles to help advance the ball.
- Add a shot at the end of the drill.
- Allow skip passes to the other side of the court.

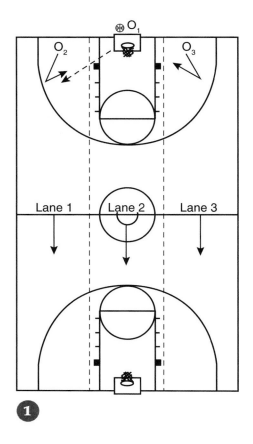

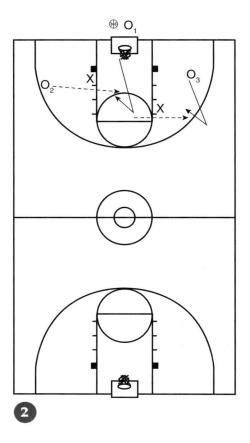

Lane 1   Lane 2   Lane 3

1

2

THREE-PLAYER CUTTING

Pat Summitt | *University of Tennessee*

Purpose

To cut without the ball and learn to develop proper spacing.

Organization

Use three offensive players.

Procedure

1. Start with the ball at the point and two wing players on either side of the lane at half-court.
2. The point player passes the ball to one of the wings and makes one of the following cuts: give-and-go, give-and-go/bump, screen away, or flare (see figures 1-4).
3. Once the point player makes a cut, the wing without the ball must react accordingly.
4. Continue passing and cutting until a shot is taken.

Coaching Points

- The passer always starts with a pass and cut.
- Players must maintain spacing and continue to react to cutting players.
- Players make at least five passes and cuts before shooting.

Variations

- Add a post player to have a post entry.
- Add a defensive post player to challenge passes.

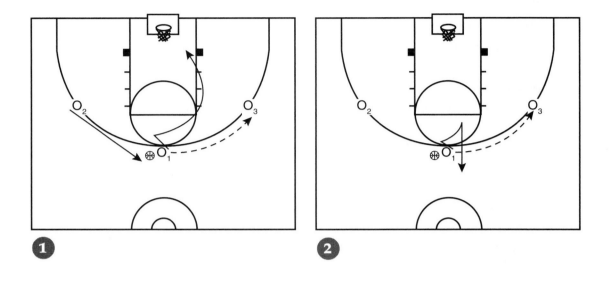

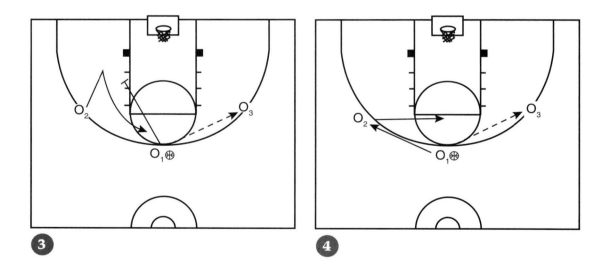

TAG

Chris Gobrecht | *Yale University*

Purpose

To teach change of speed and direction on offense and attack angles on defense.

Organization

Players work in teams of two: evaders on offense and pursuers on defense.

Procedure

1. Two teams of two step onto the court with one pursuer in each half. Both evaders start along the endline (see figure 1).
2. The first team of evaders attempts to get to the opposite endline without being tagged by the pursuers.
3. The first evader must cross half-court before the second evader may begin (see figure 2).
4. The first pursuer must start at the top of the three-point circle and may not pursue beyond half-court.
5. The second pursuer may pursue anyone who has crossed half-court and is not in the free zone, the center-court circle.
6. A tag made on either evader causes both evaders to become pursuers.

Coaching Points

- Players should keep their bodies low with their weight forward. This will help them stay balanced for quick changes of direction.
- Evaders should emphasize acceleration and lateral change of direction.
- Pursuers should emphasize sprinting to position and staying balanced.

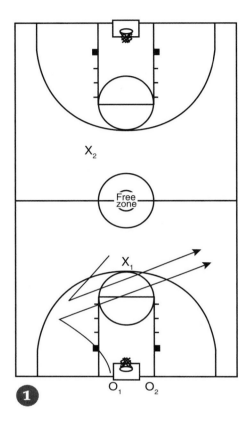

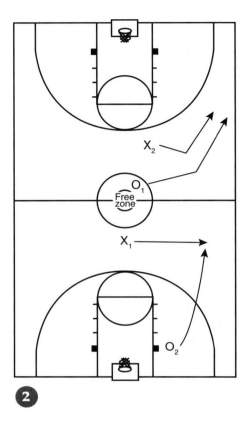

23   WRAP AND SCREEN

Trina Patterson | University of Albany

Purpose
To develop cutting, change of direction, and screening on the ball.

Organization
Players form two lines: one for the post players at the top of the key and one for the perimeter players. The perimeter player line has two balls.

Procedure
1. Each perimeter player makes a pass to the high-post player.
2. The perimeter player then makes a hard cut toward the post player (see figure 1).
3. She wraps around the post player by planting her outside foot to change direction then sets a screen on the post player.
4. The post player squares up and drives to the basket for a layup.

Coaching Points
- Perimeter players should make crisp passes to the post player and accelerate hard on the first three strides toward the post.
- Perimeter players must accelerate to position and stay balanced to set a solid screen.

Variation
Send the perimeter player to wrap and go (replace herself) at the wing while the post player squares up to drive or passes back to the perimeter (see figure 2).

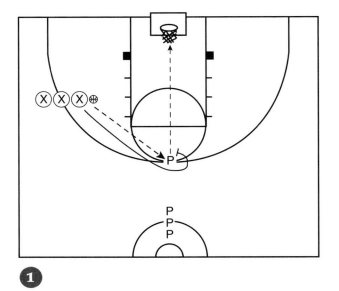

1

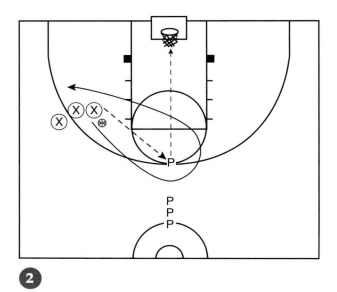

2

Trina Patterson | *University of Albany*

Purpose

To encourage players to pass and make strong cuts toward the rim without the ball.

Organization

Players form two passing lines on either side of the court on the three-point circle and two lines under the basket with the first players starting at the midpost area.

Procedure

1. The first perimeter player in each line starts with a ball on the three-point circle (see figure 1).
2. Perimeter players pass to the post player and then take one step toward the baseline.
3. The perimeter player then makes a hard cut up to the top side of the post player.
4. The post player passes to the perimeter player, who makes a layup.
5. After passing, the post player goes to the end of the midpost line.
6. The perimeter player goes to the back of the other passing line.

Coaching Points

- Players should change speed on the cut to the basket.
- Players must cut hard with the hands in catching position.
- Players on each side should alternate performing the drill so that they have space to cut.

Variation

Move perimeter player lines to the baseline for basket cuts on the bottom side of the post (see figure 2).

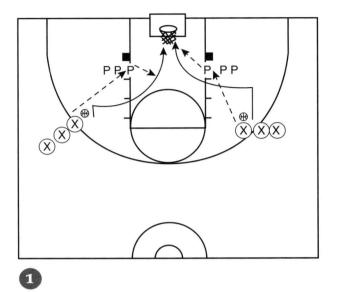

1

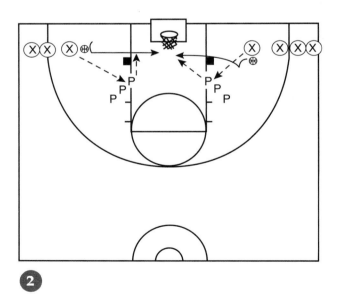

2

X-CUTTING

Trina Patterson | *University of Albany*

Purpose
To develop movement without the ball on an entry pass to the post.

Organization
Two lines of perimeter players stand outside the three-point circle. The post player starts on the ballside block; the balls start in the top line of perimeter players.

Procedure
1. The first cutter line is on the baseline; the second is along the free throw line extended.
2. The second cutter (O_4) makes a pass into the post player and steps high and away from the baseline.
   She must wait for the first cutter (O_1).
3. After O_4 passes to the post player, the first cutter cuts toward the baseline and then toward the top of the post player.

Coaching Points
- The post player may pass to either cutter or drive herself.
- The second cutter must delay her cut for the first cutter.
- Both cutters must read the post player to see if she will make a move to the basket.

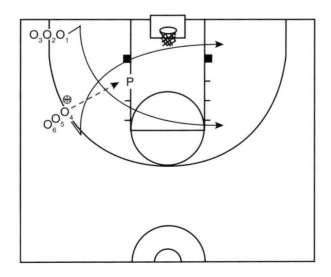

ARGENTINEAN WARM-UP

Rick Insell | *Middle Tennessee State University*

Purpose

To work on passing and catching on the move by focusing on communication and footwork.

Organization

Eight players stand around the perimeter of the half-court. Use two balls. The drill takes four to eight minutes.

Procedure

1. The drill starts when two players standing opposite each other pass to the right (or left) at the same time.
2. As soon as a player releases the ball she sprints across the floor to the opposite side and prepares for the pass.
3. Players pass the balls as quickly as possible.

Coaching Points

- Players must pay attention to footwork as they catch and pass the ball, sprint, and get in position to catch.
- Players must communicate so they don't collide in the center.
- Player should move the ball as quickly as possible and sprint to keep the drill going.
- After 30 seconds to a minute, another group comes in or a few players substitute in.

Variations

- Add pairs of players to perform passes at half-court to increase the congestion. Passes will be shorter, but it will get more involved.
- Perform the drill with eight players on the full court. The players with balls start under each basket. Two players are on the wings on both ends of the court, and two players are at half-court.

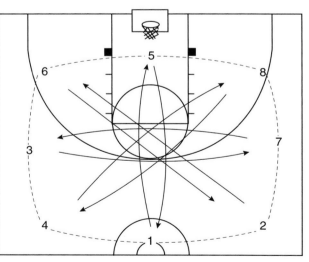

MAZE DRIBBLING

Rick Insell | *Middle Tennessee State University*

Purpose

To simulate game situations while working on dribble moves (e.g., reverse pivot, crossover, between the legs, behind the back, hesitation, in and out, stutter) repeatedly against defense.

Organization

Six defenders line up on each sideline about three feet (0.9 meter) inbounds and spread the length of the court. The rest of the team splits into two offensive groups and stands on the baseline on either side of the basket. Each group has three or four basketballs. The drill takes 4 to 10 minutes.

Procedure

1. The first offensive player in each group on the baseline begins dribbling at the first defender, who forces the ball handler to use a dribble move to get by.
2. The offensive player continues to the next defender and on down the floor. The next offensive player starts when the first offensive player gets to the second defender.

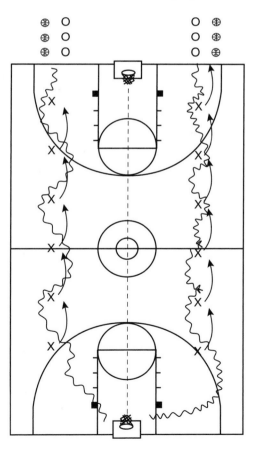

3. The defensive players move up a spot as soon as all the offensive players get by them. Once all the offensive players get by the last defender, the last offensive player to go through the line goes to the middle and passes the ball down the center to the person in line without a ball.

Coaching Points

- The offense must use different moves to get by the defense; do not allow them to repeat the same moves.
- The defensive players should force the offensive players to go in different directions as they move down the floor so that they must pay attention to what is going on in front of them.

Variation

Position a coach or manager in the center of the floor. The dribbler must pass to the coach if the coach puts her or his hands up. The dribbler gets the ball right back and continues.

28   # POST MOVES

Rick Insell | *Middle Tennessee State University*

Purpose

To allow the posts to work on footwork and moves, and guards to work on post feeds.

Organization

The entire team can participate in this half-court drill. All guards have basketballs. The drill lasts 4 to 20 minutes.

Procedure

1. Guards have basketballs on both wings, posts are posting on both blocks, and the guards feed the posts, who execute a post move.
2. Guards, after feeding the post, immediately go and get the ball out of the net and go to the other side of the floor.
3. Posts make three consecutive moves before they leave the floor and another post comes on. The order of the post moves can vary, but should include a drop step, a turn-and-shoot, and up-and-under without dribble, an up-and-under with dribble, a European, and a fake-and-shoot (faking either center or baseline).

Coaching Points

- The post must be wide and low when she posts and must explode on her move.
- Coaches determine what types of passes the guards make into the post.

Variations

- Use pads so that the posts can attack as they post up. The managers with pads can make the posts read them to make the correct move.
- Use defenders on the guards to make the entry passes more difficult.
- Have players kick out to the guards for shots and then assume rebound positioning after the guards shoot.

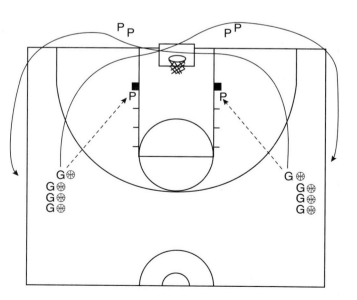

THREE LINES FULL COURT

Rick Insell ┃ *Middle Tennessee State University*

Purpose

To work on passing and catching on the move, the post cracking down on pads, and shooting perimeter transition shots.

Organization

Split the team into three lines under the basket. Guards are in the center line. Place four cones on the floor to make the players run wide. The drill is full court and lasts 8 to 20 minutes.

Procedure

1. The guard initiates the drill, and the first three players move down the floor and execute a transition sequence.
2. Once the group finishes the sequence, they get off the floor under the goal and prepare to go to the other end after all the groups have finished.
3. Players perform the following sequence as they move down the floor:

   Layup—Guard hits a post for a layup.

   Block shot—Guard hits a post for a jump shot on the block.

   Kick-out (relocate)—Guard gives the ball to a post. She dribbles down and cracks down on the pad on the block. Guard relocates and the post hits a three-pointer.

   Power skip—This is the same as a kick-out, but when the guard gets the ball, she drives to the center and kicks to the other wing for a three-pointer or a jump shot.

   Feed the post—This is the same as a power skip, except when the wing gets the ball, she feeds the post, who has moved to the ball side to post.

Coaching Points

Vary the sequence, using elements that fit into your transition game.

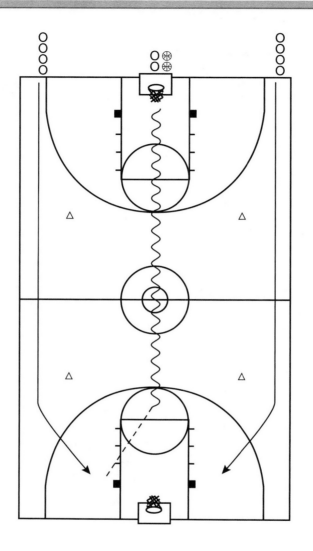

chapter 4

Dribbling Drills

Everyone handles the ball in today's game. Gone are the days when only the guards were allowed to dribble and posts were forbidden from putting the ball on the floor. Motion offenses require outstanding ballhandling skills from all five players in both half- and full-court situations. And although not every team has a player like Sue Bird or Ivory Latta to break the press, the more confident and skilled teams can handle most presses with a combination of good court awareness and purposeful dribbling.

Teams that put the ball in their most competent ball handler's hands are wise, but they also are limited in pressing and trapping situations. As the game changes and bigger players develop the ability and instinct to handle the ball in the open court, defenses are stretched and challenged to try to stop five players from advancing the ball. Skillful dribbling can neutralize a pressing defense. The following drills will help you build a solid foundation for offensive success by developing confident and skilled ball handlers—a whole team of them.

SNAP AND TOUCH

April McDivitt | University of California at Santa Barbara

Purpose
To exaggerate the importance of staying low while using a change-of-direction move.

Organization
Players stand on the baseline, each with a ball.

Procedure
1. While in an athletic stance, the player dribbles the ball two or three times about waist high on the outside of the right leg.
2. The player then uses a right-to-left crossover move, emphasizing the snap of the ball below her knees. It is important for the player to keep the ball tight to her body during the crossover. The player must catch the ball below her knee with her left hand and push the ball forward. The ball should end up in front of her left foot.
3. After snapping the ball through, her right hand touches the floor.
4. The player returns to the starting position and does the drill 10 times on each side.
5. The player continues the drill while moving. With each change of direction the player touches the floor after she snaps the ball below her knees.

Coaching Points
- The drill exaggerates how low a player must be in order to maximize her athletic ability and speed.
- The ball handler must execute the drill at world-class game speed and pound the basketball—no soft dribbles.
- The player must keep her eyes up at all times.

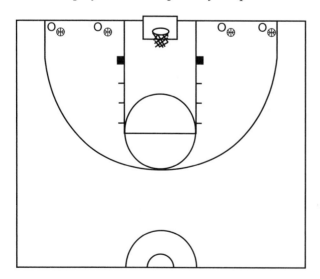

- The ball must be in front of the lead leg and tight to the body so that it doesn't slow the player down.

Variations
- Use the same drill for between-the-legs dribbling.
- Don't allow the player to move on to the next drill until she does the current drill without mistakes.

31 TWO-BALL HIGH AND LOW

April McDivitt | University of California at Santa Barbara

Purpose
To strengthen the hand, arm, and core in order to provide greater control of the basketball. Promotes eye–hand coordination and develops a feel for the ball.

Organization
Players, each with two balls, stand on the baseline.

Procedure
1. The player starts by dribbling both balls at ear level at the same time.
2. The coach calls out "low" or "high," and the ball handler pounds the basketballs to that level within one dribble and maintains dribbling both balls at the designated height until the coach calls the next command. This goes on for one minute.
3. Next, at the coach's call, the player begins a staggered dribble, where one ball will be on the floor while the other is high. The coach calls out either "high" or "low." The players pound the basketballs and change from high to low on the coach's command for one minute.

Coaching Points
- Emphasize pounding the basketball so that players gain confidence in controlling the basketball while pounding hard.
- Demand that the ball handler keep her eyes up at all times.
- Make sure players keep their core tight during the drill.
- Demand that the ball handler change levels within one dribble of your command.

Variations
- Perform the drill using two-ball V dribbles on the side of the body and two-ball crossovers in front of the body.
- As players get stronger and more comfortable with the drill, change between all four high–low combinations (same time, alternate, side V dribble, crossover) during the one-minute drill.

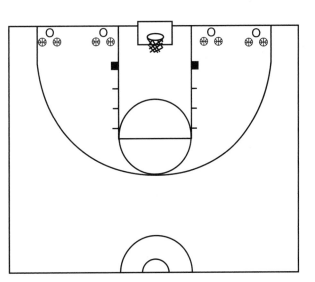

April McDivitt | *University of California at Santa Barbara*

Purpose

To gain confidence in the ability to control and handle the basketball with both hands.

Organization

Players, each with two balls, stand on the baseline.

Procedure

1. The player starts by dribbling both balls at the same time, heading to the right. After two dribbles she makes a crossover dribble with the ball in her right hand, keeping the crossover close to her body. She simultaneously executes the same crossover, but with the left hand. As a set-up after two dribbles, she switches directions and completes these repetitions in a zigzag down the court and back.

2. For the next trip down the court and back, the player dribbles both balls, heading to the right. After two dribbles, she bounces the ball in her right hand between her legs and switches the ball in her left hand to her right hand by crossing it in front of her body. She zigzags down the court and back using two dribbles between each between-the-legs move.

3. For the next trip down the court and back, the player dribbles both balls, heading to the right. After two dribbles, she takes the ball in her right hand and snaps it behind her back to her left hand, while simultaneously switching the ball from her left hand to her right hand with a front crossover move. She continues to zigzag.

4. For the final trip down and back, the player speed dribbles both balls on the floor at the same time from baseline to baseline. On the way back to the baseline, she switches to an alternating dribble. She must keep her hand behind the ball, pushing the ball out in front of her and not turning the ball over on each dribble.

Coaching Points

- Require the ball handler to perform each step without mistakes before moving on to the next step. Teach the drill from baseline to half-court. As the players gain skill and confidence, progress to baseline to baseline.
- Make sure the player keeps her eyes up at all times.
- Use just two dribbles between each change of direction so that you can gauge how well the players control where the basketball goes.

Variations

- Add an in-and-out dribble and a spin-behind-the-back two-ball dribble.
- Anything your players can do with one ball, try with two balls.
- Time how long it takes the players to complete each step of the series.

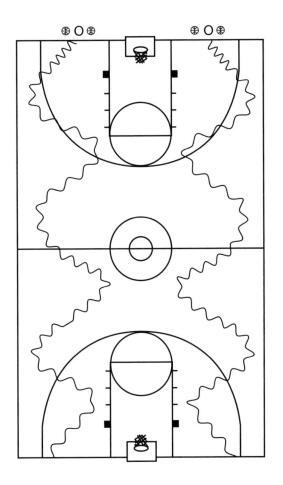

TWO-ON-ONE BALLHANDLING AGAINST PRESSURE

April McDivitt | *University of California at Santa Barbara*

Purpose

To simulate gamelike full-court pressure and improve the ball handler's ability to change direction and speed with the ball. To improve conditioning.

Organization

An offensive player is positioned at the foul line, two defenders are at the elbows, and a coach with the ball is under the basket.

Procedure

1. The coach yells "go," and the offensive player makes a cut to get open. Once the offensive player touches the ball, the play is live.
2. The two defender's goal is to steal the ball, create a turnover, or force the ballhandler to split the trap and tip the ball from behind. The defender should never get beat on the sideline side of the court.
3. The ball handler's goal is to jump-stop with two feet in the paint at the other end of the court. (No shots are taken, because the drill focuses on handling against pressure.)

Coaching Points

- Remind the ball handler to keep her eyes up at all times.
- Encourage the player to change speed and direction during the drill.
- Demand that the ball handler be the aggressor by making contact with one of the defender's outside hips (no banana cuts).
- Make it clear that this is only a drill. In a game situation, players should pass the ball to an open teammate when two defenders guard them.

Variation

Keep score. A jump stop in the paint is worth two points. A stop by the defense is worth one point.

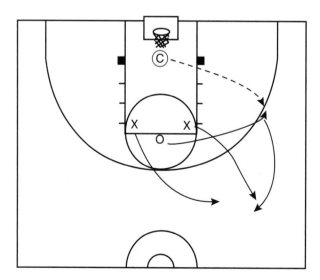

34   SPEED-DRIBBLING CHASE

Kathy Delaney-Smith | *Harvard University*

Purpose
To practice speed dribbling and to teach the defense to flick the ball away from the offensive player from behind.

Organization
Players with similar foot speed pair up. Each set of partners has a ball on the end line.

Procedure
1. The dribbler takes two steps in front of the defensive partner. The dribbler may not switch her dribbling hand once she starts.
2. The defensive player tries to beat the dribbler to the other end line or to flick the ball from behind.
3. Players switch roles and return from the opposite end line.

Coaching Points
- The dribbler should use her lead for advantage.
- The defender should try to overcome the lead with speed or by properly timing her defensive flick.

Variation
The coach may adjust the dribbler's lead to make it competitive.

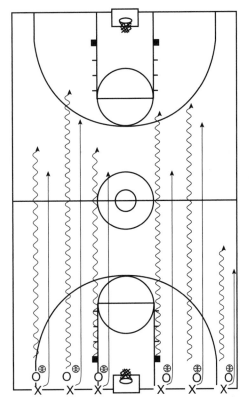

HERDING

Wendy Larry | *Old Dominion University*

Purpose

To maintain dribble and attempt to dribble out of a trap.

Organization

One line of offensive players stands at the foul line, facing the opposite basket; each person in line has a ball. A line of defensive players stands on the right sideline and another on the left sideline, both at half-court.

Procedure

1. The first offensive player in line (O_1) begins dribbling toward the opposite basket.
2. The first defender from each line at half-court approaches the dribbler.
3. The two defenders attempt to "herd" the dribbler toward the sideline, where they can trap her.
4. The player must attempt to avoid the trap with her dribble and to score on the two defenders.
5. If the player scores or picks up her dribble without a shot or if the defense steals the ball, everyone goes to the back of the line they came from and the next three players begin.

Coaching Points

- Remind players to keep their heads up while dribbling.
- Teach players to avoid traps by backing out of a trap with the dribble, splitting the trap with the dribble, or driving by the trap before it can be set.
- Emphasize that a player is not expected to beat the trap and score every time.

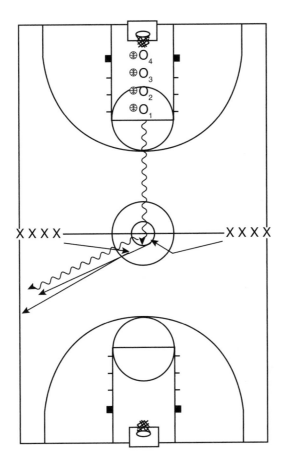

Rene Portland | *Penn State University*

Purpose

To develop ballhandling skills and skills in reading defense, passing, and penetrating with the ball.

Organization

Players stand in three lines. A coach at midcourt has the ball.

Procedure

1. Players form two lines at midcourt. The line closest to the sideline is on offense. The line closest to the jump circle is on defense. A third line is on the baseline on the other side of the basket from the other two lines.
2. From midcourt, a coach or manager throws the ball toward the sideline in front of the offensive player (see figure 1).
3. Player O_1 receives the ball and goes to the basket to score. She reads the defense and decides whether to go strong for a layup or pull up for a jump shot.
4. The defensive player leaves as soon as the ball is thrown. She tries to chase and catch the offensive player in order to stop her from scoring.
5. As soon as player O_1 puts up a shot (make or miss), she retreats down the court on defense. The defensive player then moves to the opposite wing to become the outlet player. The first person in the line along the baseline (O_4) steps onto the court, rebounds the ball, and makes an outlet pass. The drill continues with a two-on-one break in the opposite direction (see figure 2).

Coaching Points

- For continuous play, carry out the two-on-one break on the half of the court opposite the one-on-one. The two-on-one can then widen once it reaches half-court to use the full half of the court.
- As the two-on-one part of the drill continues, begin a new set of players in the one-on-one part of the drill.

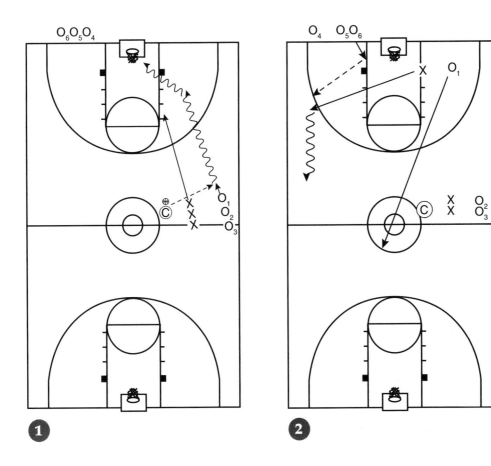

Brenda Frese | *University of Maryland*

Purpose

To improve ballhandling for better control and possession dribbling.

Organization

Players stand in staggered lines in the center of the floor facing the coach. Each player has a ball and stands at least an arm's length from the other players. The coach should have a good view of each player.

Procedure

1. Players start with ball in the right hand, feet shoulder-width apart, knees bent, and head up. They swing the ball in front of the feet, using good hand control and a continuous exaggerated inside-out motion. The ball should not bounce higher than the knee. After 30 seconds, the players switch to the left hand.

2. With the ball in the right hand, right foot forward, knees bent, and head up, players swing the ball on the right side of the right leg. The ball should not bounce higher than the knee. After 30 seconds, players switch to the left hand, put the left foot forward, and swing the ball on the side of the left leg.

3. Players take a long stride forward with the right foot. The legs stay stationary in this position with the knees bent. The head is up. Players dribble the ball from the left hand to the right hand back and forth between the legs. After 30 seconds, players put the left leg forward and repeat.

4. With the feet a little more than shoulder-width apart, knees bent, and the head up, players use a low dribble to weave the ball in a figure-8 motion between the legs using both hands and a total of five dribbles. After 30 seconds, players repeat in the opposite direction.

5. Players execute a figure-8 using three dribbles. After 30 seconds, players repeat in the opposite direction.

6. Players execute a figure-8 using one dribble. After 30 seconds, players repeat in the opposite direction.

7. With the feet shoulder-width apart, knees slightly bent, and head up, players dribble the ball behind the back from right hand to left hand for 30 seconds.

Coaching Points

- Dribbles should stay at knee level or below.
- Players should keep the head up, eyes forward, and knees bent.
- Once players master control, they should work on speed.
- Players should pound the ball on the ground with each dribble, practicing good control.

Variation

Beginners can use an extra dribble when dribbling between the legs and behind the back.

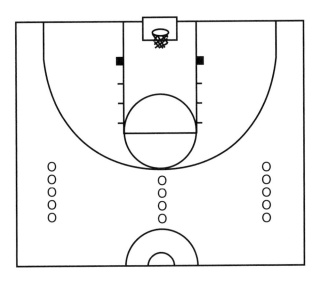

Brenda Frese | *University of Maryland*

Purpose

To improve control while dribbling and master full-speed ballhandling while changing directions. To incorporate ballhandling moves into finishing layups.

Organization

Players form a line at the baseline, facing the half-court. Each player has a ball. A coach stands between the top of the key and the half-court circle to view the drill. A second coach stands at the three-point line, as a token defender.

Procedure

1. Players start one at a time dribbling up the sideline. They turn left and dribble across the half-court line to the other sideline. Players wait until the person in front of them is halfway up the sideline before starting. They finish by heading to the basket to shoot a right-handed layup and then return to the back of the line. Players follow this pattern four times using the following ballhandling moves.

   Crossover—The player dribbles up the sideline, using the crossover move every third dribble until she reaches half-court. She turns left and dribbles down the half-court line using the crossover move with every other dribble. At the sideline, she turns left to face the basket. With the ball in her left hand she speed dribbles to the coach at the three-point line and uses the crossover move to her right to finish with a right-handed layup.

   In-and-out—The player dribbles with her right hand up the sideline, using an in-and-out move every third dribble. At half-court she turns left and, still dribbling with her right hand, uses the in-and-out move every other dribble. At the sideline, she turns left and faces the basket. With the ball still in her right hand, she speed dribbles to the coach at the three-point line, makes the in-and-out move, and finishes with a right-handed layup.

   Between-the-legs—The player dribbles up the sideline and takes the ball between her legs every third dribble, and on ever other dribble across the half-court line. At the other sideline, she faces the basket with the ball in her left hand and speed dribbles to the coach at the three-point line, she takes the ball between the legs and finishes with a right-handed layup.

   Behind-the-back—The player follows the same format as in the other three sequences, but uses a behind-the-back move.

2. Once all the players have finished all four moves, the line moves to the other corner and repeats the drill in a clockwise direction, finishing with a left-handed layup.

Coaching Points

- Players should keep the dribble low and the head up.
- Players should dribble as fast as they can while maintaining control and finish strong with the layup.

Variation

More advanced players can use the ballhandling move on every dribble when going across half-court.

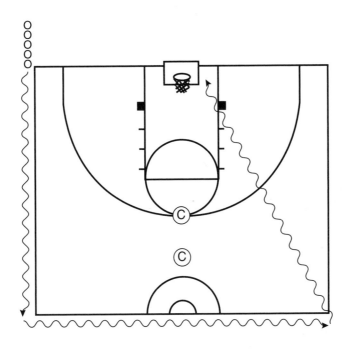

Brenda Frese | University of Maryland

Purpose

To improve control and speed while handling the basketball.

Organization

Players form three lines at half-court, facing the basket. The player at the front of the line has a ball. Six cones are set in front of each line and lead to the basket.

Procedure

1. Players weave through the cones at full speed and maintain control using the following moves: crossover, between-the-legs, and behind-the-back.
2. The player in the front of the line on the right weaves through the cones using the designated move and finishes with a right-handed layup. She then moves to the back of the middle line.
3. Once she is done, the player at the front of the middle line weaves through the cones, performing the same move and finishing with a layup over the front of the rim. She then moves to the back of the left line.
4. When she is done, the player in the front of the left line weaves through her set of cones and finishes with a left-handed layup. She then goes to the back of the right line.

Coaching Points

- Players should keep the dribble low.
- Players must keep the head up and eyes forward.
- Once players master control, they should work on speed.
- Players should pound the ball on the ground with each dribble, practicing control.
- Players should protect the back with the opposite hand.

Variation

Beginners use fewer cones spaced farther apart.

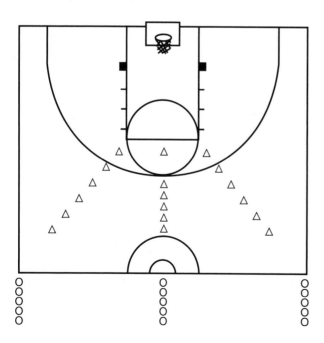

40 POSSESSION DRIBBLING

Brenda Frese | University of Maryland

Purpose
To improve possession dribbling and delivering a pass to the post while being closely guarded by a defender.

Organization
Players form one line on each side of the court at the wing area (foul line extended at the three-point line). Each line has one ball. One coach stands on each block.

Procedure
1. The first person in the line is the defender, and the second person in the line has the ball on offense. While being closely guarded, the offensive player maintains her dribble and keeps her head up.
2. The offensive player can only move one step to the left or right.
3. The defender tries to steal the ball and make it difficult for the offensive player to see the coach on the block.
4. When the coach on the block puts a hand out to receive a pass, the offensive player immediately delivers a bounce pass around the defensive player to the coach.
5. The rotation for the drill is offense to defense, and defense to the back of the opposite line.

Coaching Points
- The dribble should stay low.
- Players should keep the head up and eyes forward.
- Players should protect the ball with the opposite hand.
- Players should pound the ball into the ground with each dribble, practicing control.
- Players should deliver the pass with speed and efficiency.

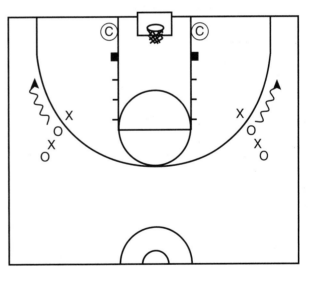

Variation
For beginners, the defender plays token defense.

chapter 5

Passing Drills

The no-look passes of Ticha Penicheiro, Nykesha Sales, and Becky Hammon bring the crowds to their feet—and sometimes cause their coaches to squirm in their seats. But the skillful passer understands when and where to deliver a pass so it leads to a scoring opportunity. Teams that drill on passing focus on eye contact, verbal communication, and, of course, timing.

For open-court teams, passing in transition is an art form. The eye contact, communication, and accuracy of passing in the open court have put a stamp on the women's game; it is what makes the game so popular. When John Wooden comments that "the best pure basketball I see today is among the better women's teams," what more needs to be said? Great passing is the cornerstone of unselfish team play. It builds confidence in all players and encourages communication. The following drills will help you build each player's confidence and skill so that she can enjoy the thrill of a great assist.

SIX-PASSER FAST BREAK

Tara VanDerveer | *Stanford University*

Purpose
To practice full-court passing, layups, and conditioning.

Organization
Use four balls (two at each end of the court), six passers, and six shooters.

Procedure
1. At least three shooters start on opposite ends of the court.
2. Three stationary passers are positioned down each side of the court.
3. The first shooter at each end starts at the same time by passing to the first target (passer) on her side—no dribbles.
4. The shooter continues down the court, passing to the next target (passer) on her side without dribbling.
5. The shooter shoots a layup and gets in line at the other end.
6. The drill is continuous. Start with one and a half minutes and work up to two minutes on each side. Switch passers and shooters after each side is done.

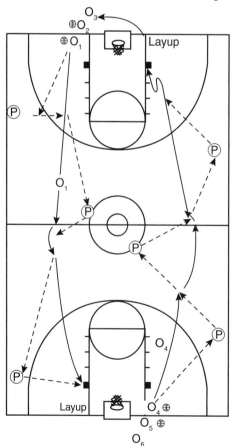

Coaching Points
- Players may not dribble.
- Players should provide good targets and sharp passes.
- Players should sprint the floor and concentrate on finishing layups.
- Passers and shooters switch after time expires.

Variation
Keep track of baskets and make it competitive.

TWO-END LAYUPS

Tara VanDerveer | *Stanford University*

Purpose

To develop transition passing skills and conditioning.

Organization

A shooting line and outlet are on one wing. A rebounding line is on the opposite side of the court. Two balls are in the shooting line, and a rack of balls is at half-court with the coach.

Procedure

1. The first shooter (O_1) passes across to the first person in the rebounding line (O_6) then receives a pass back for a layup.
2. The rebounder rebounds and passes to the outlet player (X); then the passer (O_6) becomes the outlet player.
3. The outlet player (X) passes to the next shooter (O_2) and goes to the end of the shooting line.
4. After the layup, the shooter sprints down the sideline, receives a ball from the coach, scores at the opposite end, and then dribbles up to the ball rack and fills the rebounding line.

Coaching Points

- Players should make sharp passes.
- Players should concentrate and finish layups on both ends.
- Players should sprint the floor.

Variation

Give every player in the shooting line a ball and take away the rack and passer. The rebounder dribbles the length of the floor for a layup and then dribbles back to the shooting line.

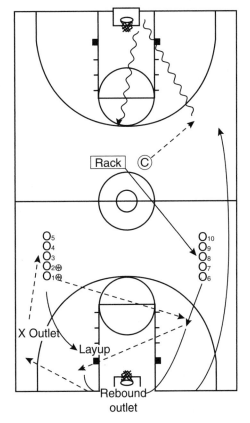

THREE WEAVE WITH TRAILER

Rene Portland | Penn State University

Purpose

To improve passing skills and conditioning and to practice transitions up and down the floor.

Organization

Players divide into four lines along the baseline. Either outside line can be designated as the "trailer" line. The first person in one of the other three lines has the ball.

Procedure

1. The first person in the trailer line (O_1) sprints down the floor. The other three players weave down the floor.
2. Once the trailer reaches the hash mark in the frontcourt, she cuts at a 45-degree angle toward the basket, calling for the ball.
3. Players in the weave may pass the ball no more than three times before hitting the trailer for a layup.

4. The trailer then sprints up the opposite sideline while the same weave continues back down the floor.
5. The trailer must make two consecutive layups before that group can step off the court.

Coaching Points

- The ball may not hit the floor at any time, either from a pass or coming out of the net.
- Passes should be crisp, and players should lead teammates with their passes.

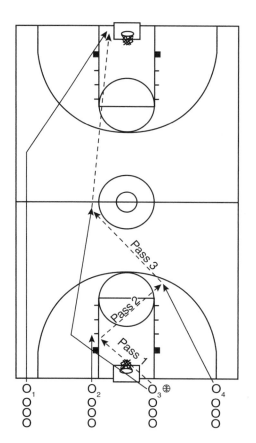

OLYMPIC PASSING

Joe McKeown | George Washington University

Purpose

To improve passing in transition, shooting while on the fast break, filling lanes, and conditioning.

Organization

Three players start at half-court with a ball in the middle; four more players start at the baselines, two on each end and each with a ball.

Procedure

1. Three players start at half-court.
2. They attack three-on-zero and make a layup.
3. The passer (P_2) and nonshooter (P_1) receive passes from the baseline passers (O_1 and O_4) and shoot game shots. The two baseline passers and the layup shooter (P_3) then attack three-on-zero to the other end of court with two baseline passers, making passes to the passer and nonshooter from the second group. This is a continuous drill.

Coaching Points

- Players should run the lanes hard and hustle.
- The ball should not hit the floor.
- Players should shoot game shots (e.g., three-pointers, post moves).
- Players should try to make 30 shots in three minutes.

Variation

Add defense.

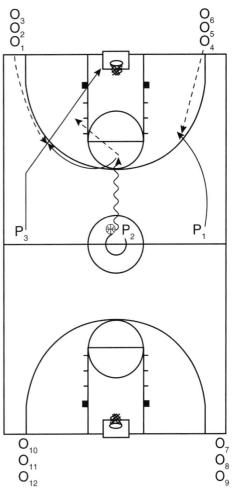

REBOUND, OUTLET, LONG

Rene Portland | *Penn State University*

Purpose

To practice fast-break situations and improve passing skills and conditioning.

Organization

Players divide into three lines on the baseline. The first person in the middle line has a ball. A coach stands at either elbow on the far end of the court.

Procedure

1. The ball starts in the middle line. The player with the ball passes to the line opposite of where the coach is to begin the drill (in figure 1, O_2 passes to O_1).
2. Player O_1 then passes the ball back to O_2. Meanwhile, O_3 sprints the length of the floor. When O_3 reaches the opposite free throw lane, O_2 passes the ball to her for a layup.
3. After completing the pass, O_2 sprints toward the foul line, circles the coach, and sprints back down the floor. After finishing the layup, O_3 moves to the outlet position on the opposite side of the floor. Player O_1 sprints the floor, rebounds the ball, and outlets to O_3 (see figure 2).
4. Player O_3 then returns the pass to O_1. Player O_1 throws a long pass to O_2 for a layup.
5. The next group takes the ball out of the net and the drill continues.

Coaching Points

- Players should take all rebounds directly out of the net. The ball should not hit the floor.
- Players should not throw long passes directly at the receiver. Instead, they should throw them ahead of the receiver, thus leading the player into the layup.

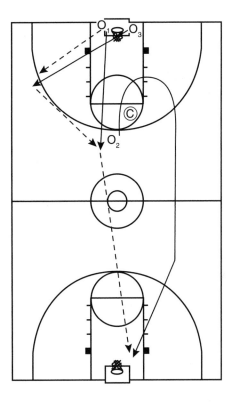

1

2

Kay Yow | *North Carolina State University*

Purpose

To attempt 25 layups in two minutes. Players can promote good communication skills by calling out each receiver's name during this drill.

Organization

Split the team evenly on each end and form three lines under each end basket. Use four balls.

Procedure

1. The ball begins in the middle line. On a signal, player B passes to player A, who is sprinting along the sideline. Player A passes back to player B in the middle. Player B passes ahead to player C, who is sprinting along the other sideline. Player C shoots a layup.

2. Player B, after passing for the layup, sprints to slap the hand of a waiting teammate (O_2), who has one foot on the end line. Player B then sprints to fill the sideline to receive the outlet pass from player A. Player C curls out to the opposite sideline, and player A rebounds and outlets to player B. The drill continues back down in the same manner—pass to the sideline, to the middle, and to the sideline for a layup by player C (see figure 1).

3. When the first group has shot their first layup and crosses half-court on their return trip, the first three players on that end line (O_1, O_2, and O_3) follow up the court with the same passing pattern—sideline, middle, sideline for a layup. Again, the shooter (O_1) curls out to the sideline opposite the passer (O_2), who has slapped hands with a teammate (E) on that end. The rebounder (O_3) turns this group (O_1, O_2, and O_3) around, and they head back down: sideline, middle, sideline, layup. When they get to half-court, the next group (D, E, and F) begins (see figure 2).

4. The drill continues for two minutes. The goal is to make 25 layups.

Coaching Points

- Players should use sharp, quick passes and provide good hand targets.
- All players should sprint at game speed.
- Players may not walk with the ball. They can take a dribble if needed before passing or before shooting the layup.

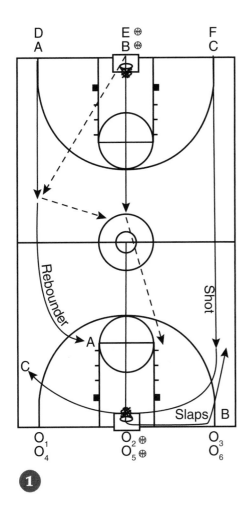

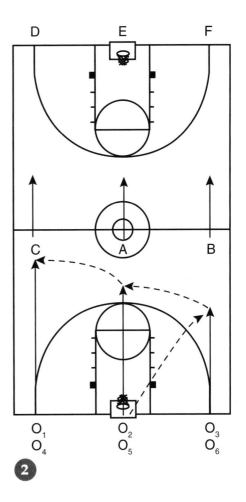

PASSING AND SHOOTING

Bernadette Mattox | WNBA's Connecticut Sun

Purpose
To improve passing, cutting, and communication skills.

Organization
Use at least nine players in three lines; each player on the baseline has a ball.

Procedure
1. Player O_1 dribbles up the sideline with her outside hand.
2. Player O_4 steps in to receive the pass from player O_1, then immediately passes to player O_7.
3. Player O_7 passes to player O_4, who has cut to the basket for a layup or jumper.
4. Player O_1 goes to the second line, player O_4 goes to the third line, and player O_7 rebounds and goes to the first line.

Coaching Points
- Players should make crisp passes.
- Players should call for the ball, meet the pass, and provide targets.

Variation
Have the players vary where they shoot from.

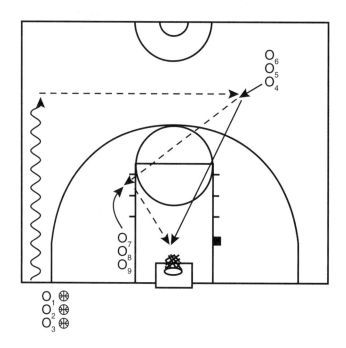

48   PIVOT AND PASS

Chris Long | *Louisiana Tech University*

Purpose
To teach a variety of passes and proper footwork while passing. Players also learn to catch the ball while moving.

Organization
Players are paired up and scattered across the court. Each pair has one basketball. Use the out-of-bounds areas if more space is needed.

Procedure
1. Players should spread out so there are 8 to 10 feet (2.5 to 3 meters) between each pair. Player 1, who has the basketball, begins pivoting and faking passes while her partner moves in a semicircle.
2. Once player 1 with the ball has made two or three pivots and pass fakes, she passes to her partner.
3. Player 2 pivots and pass-fakes while player 1 moves a bit so she isn't standing still.

Coaching Points
- Encourage movement by both players.
- Encourage players to use their right pivot foot several times and their left pivot foot several times.
- Demand that the player with ball make gamelike fakes, jabs, and passes. Don't allow sloppiness.
- Insist that the player with ball pass-fake and pivot as if she were being guarded. This encourages wraparound passes with both hands and better pass fakes.

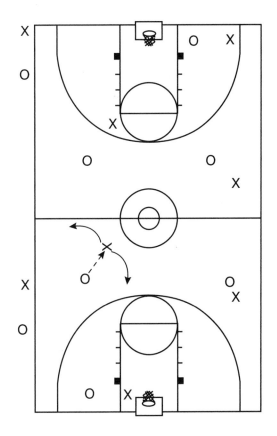

MAN IN THE MIDDLE

Chris Long | *Louisiana Tech University*

Purpose

To work on being strong with the basketball in order to make accurate passes while being pressured defensively. To improve quickness and reaction time to the basketball.

Organization

Split players into groups of three. An offensive player stands at each end of the foul line. One of the offensive players has a ball. The third player is between them and is on defense. If the groups are uneven, a manager or coach can step in.

Procedure

1. Player X_1 guards O_1 and tries to deflect the pass from O_1 to O_2.
2. Player O_1 works on ball fakes and steps through the defense to make the pass.
3. When O_2 receives the ball, X_1 runs over to contest O_2's pass back to O_1. Player O_2 must hold the ball for two seconds before passing it back to O_1.
4. Player X_1 stays in the middle and defends both passes until she gets a deflection.
5. Once X_1 gets a deflection, she rotates out to become an offensive player. The player that made the bad pass rotates in on defense.

Coaching Points

- Players that are passing the basketball should be in triple-threat position and ready to make a sharp pass.
- The offensive passers should not drift outside of the foul lane as the drill continues. The space between the passers and defender should be tight, which makes it more difficult for the passers.

Variations

- Incorporate different passes, such as curl pass, hook pass, and step through.
- Make the defender stay in the middle until five passes are thrown.

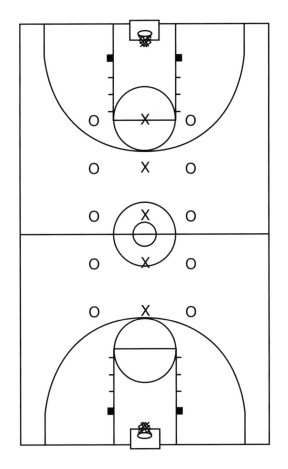

Chris Long | *Louisiana Tech University*

Purpose

To work on proper passing techniques, receiving a pass with proper footwork so that a player is ready to shoot, and maintaining balance during pivoting and passing.

Organization

The drill works best with 12 or more players (see variations for a drill with fewer players). Players form four lines at the corners of an imaginary square with sides 15 to 17 feet (4.6 to 5.2 meters) long. Place a cone in the middle of the square. Use one basketball initially. Use four balls once players have mastered the drill.

Procedure

1. Player 1 begins by throwing a two-hand chest pass to player 2 and running to the back of player 2's line.
2. Player 2 anticipates the pass and steps toward player 1 with her inside foot (the foot closest to the middle of the square as she faces the passer) as she receives the ball.
3. As player 2 receives the pass, she pivots on her inside foot and squares her body toward the cone in the middle of the square, faking a shot toward the cone.
4. After the shot fake, player 2 pivots across her body, stepping toward player 3 to make a chest pass, and runs to the back of player 3's line.
5. Player 3 receives the pass, shot-fakes and passes to player 4. Player 4 receives the pass, shot-fakes, and passes to the line where player 1 originally started.
6. Continue the drill until each player has completed five or six repetitions. Then switch the direction of the pass. Players now use the other foot as their inside, or pivot, foot.

Coaching Points

- Receivers must have their hands ready to catch and shoot and must play low, in a good athletic stance, when stepping toward the passer.
- On the catch, players should point the toe of their inside foot, or pivot foot, toward the cone.
- The catch, pivot, and shot fake should occur in one fluid movement.
- Players should keep the knees bent and hips flexed during the catch, pivot, and shot fake so that they can maintain balance when they pivot to cross over to make the pass to the next line.

Variations

- If you have fewer than 12 players, put the players in groups of four. They will not rotate to the next line after passing.
- Have players throw the following passes: bounce pass, wraparound bounce pass, and outside-hand chest pass, which is great for strengthening a player's weak hand.
- Add more basketballs to speed it up. Up to four balls are possible with the 12-person drill. Use no more than two for a four-player group.
- Put a dummy defense on each player to make the offense protect the ball while faking shots and making passes.

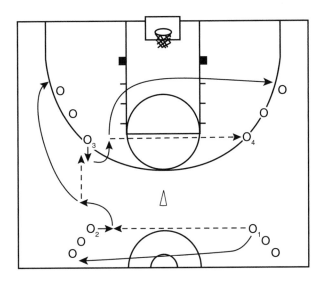

51   FEED THE POST

Chris Long | *Louisiana Tech University*

Purpose

To perfect perimeter players' entry passing to posts while working on positioning, timing, and accuracy. It is also a great warm-up drill in the half-court.

Organization

Perimeter players form two lines at the foul line extended on both sides of the floor. Two lines of post players are under the basket. Each perimeter player has a basketball. Two managers play dummy defense on the perimeter players.

Procedure

1. The post players on each side of the floor (O_3 and O_4) step out and post up above the first marker (see figure 1).
2. The perimeter players on each side of the floor (O_1 and O_2) are in a triple threat and assume an athletic stance. The dummy defense (Xs) matches up with a perimeter player on each side of the floor.
3. The perimeter player uses ball fakes and pass fakes and then makes an entry pass to the post, who is calling for the ball.
4. The post player catches and chins the ball, makes a post move, and scores. The post player rebounds her own shot and hands the ball to the perimeter player, who has followed the entry pass and crashed the board.
5. Each perimeter player receives the ball back from the post player and then proceeds to the back of the perimeter line on the opposite side of the floor. Post players switch lines under the basket after each repetition.

Coaching Points

- Demand solid positioning and strength with the ball from perimeter players entering the ball to the post.
- Remind post players to show a distinct target.
- Encourage players to practice gamelike ball fakes to help prevent careless turnovers in game situations.
- Teach perimeter players to know exactly where teammates prefer to catch the ball and to put them in a position to catch and score.

Variations

- Add live defense on perimeter players.
- Have perimeter players make the entry pass and relocate on the same side of the floor (see figure 2).
- Have perimeter players make the entry pass and relocate to the elbow, while the post player on the opposite block pivots and makes a strong overhead pass to the perimeter players. Perimeter players catch while in a good stance and shoot the basketball (inside backside) (see figure 3).

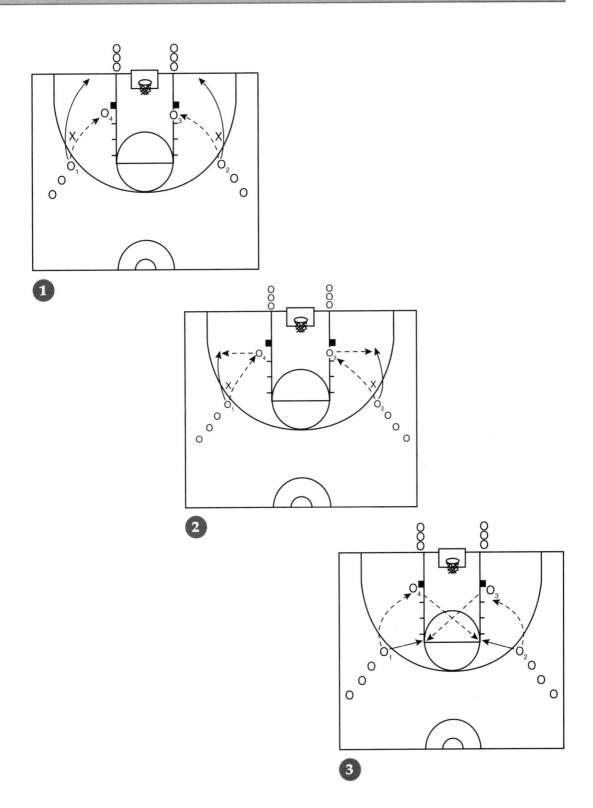

chapter 6

Offensive Screening Drills

With few exceptions in today's game, players do not just "get open"; they have to work to earn their shots. Motion offenses rely heavily on excellent screening execution and getting the ball to their scorers in scoring position. Players like Sue Bird and Sheryl Swoopes have mastered the art of getting open off their teammates' screens.

In this chapter are great breakdowns from top coaches and excellent teaching tips on how to build screening drills into your live competitive action. Maybe you do not have a great one-on-one player who can create a scoring opportunity for herself, but you can develop the ability for all players to work for opportunities through effective screens.

BASIC SCREEN

Kay Yow | *North Carolina State University*

Purpose

To teach players the proper stance and body position for screening.

Organization

Split the team into three lines on the end line.

Procedure

1. On the whistle, the first three players sprint to the free throw lane, pop their feet on a jump stop with their knees flexed, bodies low, and arms crossed tightly over their chests in a screening stance. They should maintain balance until the whistle sounds to continue.
2. At the next whistle, the first three players sprint to half-court and screen again while the next three in line sprint to the free throw lane and screen.
3. The drill continues until all players have executed a proper screening stance in both free throw lanes and at midcourt.

Coaching Point

Players must remain low and maintain balance, with their arms crossed and head and eyes up.

Variation

Screeners perform a roll, a step back, or a step to after each screen.

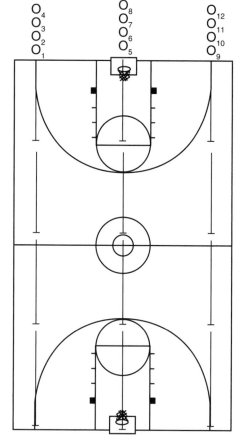

53

DOWN SCREEN

Carol Ross | *University of Mississippi*

Purpose

To teach proper technique for setting a down screen.

Organization

Use a minimum three players with one ball.

Procedure

1. A coach starts with the ball at the top.
2. One player starts on the wing, and one player starts on the block.
3. The first player sets a down screen for the second player on the block.
4. The second player sets up her cut and uses the screen. She looks to score after using the screen.
5. The first player opens up and rolls to the ball after contact has been made.

Coaching Points

- On a down screen, the screener's back should angle away from the basket.
- The screener must stay low and maintain a wide, strong base.
- The screener should always open up (roll) to the ball after contact has been made so that she becomes a threat to score. This is especially important against a switching defense.

Variations

- Add defenders and build up to two-on-two.
- Sometimes allow only the screener (O_1) to score.

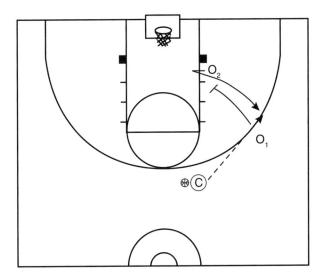

CURL OR FLARE

Kay Yow | *North Carolina State University*

Purpose

To teach players the techniques of reading and using a down screen for a curl cut, a flare, or a backdoor cut.

Organization

Use one ball, a manager/defender, and a passer/coach. Split players into three lines: one at the top of the key, one on one wing, and a third under the basket. The passer/coach begins on the opposite wing with the ball. The defender begins on the player under the basket.

Procedure

1. The drill begins as the passer/coach passes up to the top. The player under the basket cuts out and prepares to use a down screen on her defender from the wing. The player using the screen must watch her defender reading her defender's position.
2. If her defender trails behind her or is caught by the screen, the offensive player accelerates at the point of the screen and curls around it, receiving the pass from the passer and scoring (see figure 1).
3. If her defender goes behind the screen, the offensive player stops, cuts out from the screen, and flares back. The screener needs to pivot and rescreen. The passer throws an overhead pass to the flaring offensive player. An open shot or quick penetration should result (see figure 2). (If the defender hustles around the screen before the pass is made, the offensive player should cut backdoor for a pass from the top.)
4. After the first three players execute, the next three step up. The defender remains the same. Player rotation is from under the basket to the wing, from the wing to the top, and from the top to under the basket.

Coaching Points

- The player using the screen for a flare should push off her teammate with both hands in the small of the back, looking for a possible rescreen.
- Players should cut off the screen shoulder to shoulder and curl tightly around it.
- Players should walk or jog to set up the defender to use the screen, then accelerate at the point of the screen.
- The screener can either screen an area or a player. When screening an area, she should set the screen approximately half the distance between the ball and the player to be screened.

Variation

When first teaching this concept, instruct the defender where to go on the screen. For example, have the defender go behind or under the screen consecutively before changing.

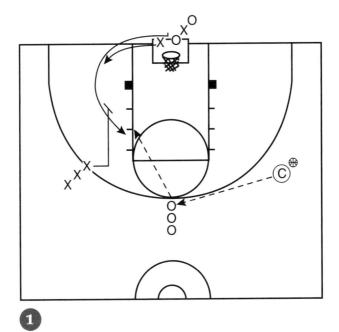

1

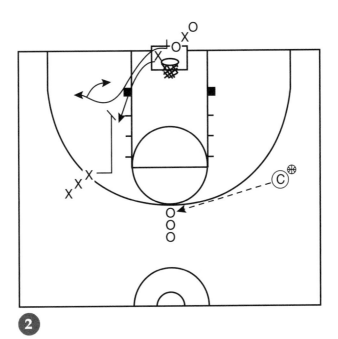

2

55   TWO-PLAYER SCREENING AND SHOOTING

Kay Yow | North Carolina State University

Purpose

To teach players the techniques of reading and using screens to cut high for a shot, to curl close for a layup, or to fake using the screen and cut backdoor.

Organization

Use the entire team with a passer and one ball. Split players into two lines: one line at the top of the key, the other line on a wing. A passer/coach is positioned on the other wing.

Procedure

1. The first player in the line on the key starts with the ball; she passes to the coach, steps toward the pass, and then screens away for the first player on the wing (see figure 1).
2. While the second pass is being made, the wing player steps toward the baseline (setting up her defender) and cuts off the screen for a jump shot. The screener rolls to the basket for the rebound.
3. The drill continues with the next two players in line.
4. The next series has the same alignment. This time the player using the screen cuts to the basket for a layup. The screener steps back away from the cutter. The coach can hit either the cutter to the basket or the screener stepping out (see figure 2).
5. The last series in the set has the player using the screen to fake up as if cutting by the screen but then cutting to the basket on a backdoor cut. The screener reads that cut and steps to the ball (see figure 3). The coach can hit either player.

Coaching Points

- Players using the screen should set up their defenders by stepping away from the screen first.
- Players should always accelerate at the point of the screen. Cut shoulder to shoulder on the curl cut.
- Screeners should position themselves in a balanced stance and keep their knees flexed, especially as they move to roll.

Variations

- Run the drill to both sides of the floor.
- Add defense on both lines.

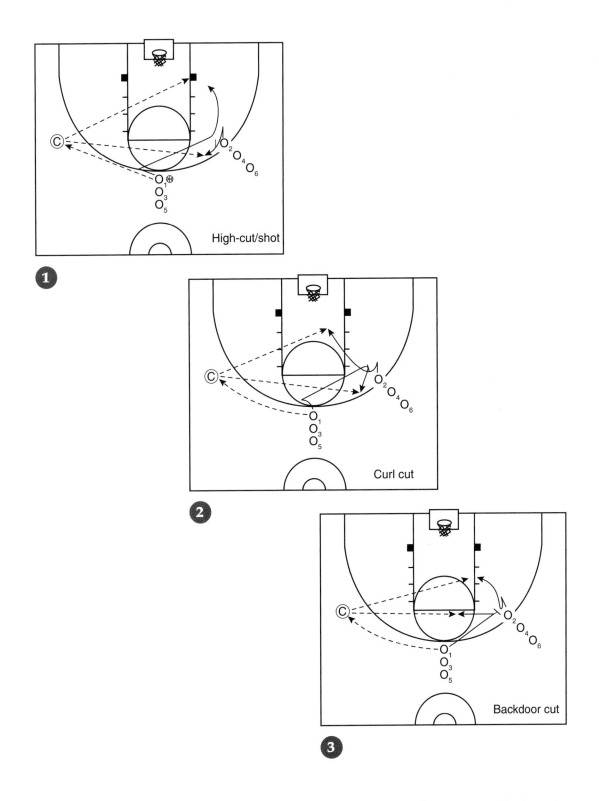

1

High-cut/shot

2

Curl cut

3

Backdoor cut

READ THE DEFENSE

Carol Ross | *University of Mississippi*

Purpose

To teach players how to read the defense and use the down screen.

Organization

Use a coach and two players and one ball.

Procedure

1. A coach starts with the ball at the top.
2. One player starts on the block with a defender, and one player starts on the wing without defense.
3. The wing player sets a down screen for the player on the block.
4. The player on the block reads the defense, sets up her defender, and makes the appropriate cut: pop-up, curl, flare, or back cut (see figures 1-4).

Coaching Points

- Players use a pop-up cut if the defender runs directly into the screen.
- Players use a curl cut if the defender is trailing or gets caught trying to get over the top of the screen.
- Players use a flare cut if the defender tries to go behind the screen and beat the cutter to her spot.
- Players use a back cut if the defender cheats up higher than the screen.
- The cutter must watch her defender, not the ball, when trying to determine which cut to make.

Variation

Add defenders and build up to two on two.

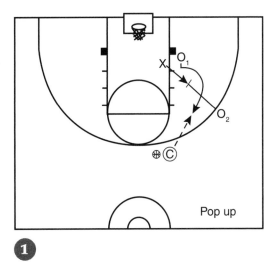

Pop up

1

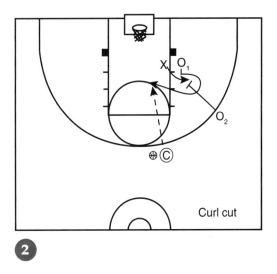

Curl cut

2

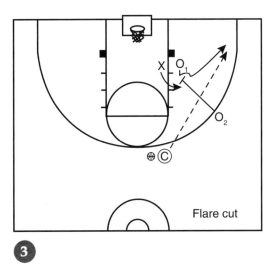

Flare cut

3

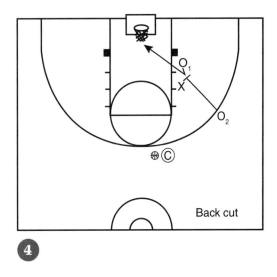

Back cut

4

BACK SCREEN

Carol Ross | *University of Mississippi*

Purpose

To teach proper technique for setting a back screen.

Organization

Use a coach and two players and one ball.

Procedure

1. The coach starts with the ball at the top.
2. One player starts on the wing, and one starts on the block.
3. The player on the block sets a back screen for the wing player.
4. The wing player sets up her cut and uses the screen. She attempts to score after using the screen and receiving a pass from the coach.
5. The player on the block steps (roll) toward the ball after contact has been made on the screen.

Coaching Points

*   On a back screen, the screener's back should angle toward the basket.
*   The screener must stay low and maintain a wide, strong base.
*   The screener should always step (roll) toward the ball after contact has been made so that she becomes a threat to score. This is especially important against a switching defense.

Variation

Add defenders and build up to two on two.

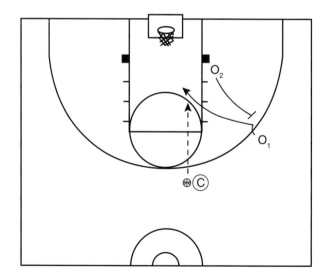

PICK-AND-ROLL

Carol Ross | *University of Mississippi*

Purpose

To teach proper technique for setting a screen on the ball.

Organization

Use a minimum of three players with one ball.

Procedure

1. The first player starts on the wing with the ball.
2. The second player starts on a ballside block and steps out to set a screen on the ball.
3. The first player sets up her defender by jabbing opposite to the direction she's going.
4. The second player rolls open to the basket after contact has been made.
5. The first player comes off the screen looking to score or pass to the second player.

Coaching Points

- The screener must stay low and maintain a wide, strong base.
- The screener must remain stationary until contact is made.
- The screener rolls to the basket after contact is made, calls for the ball, and shows the ball handler a big target.

Variations

- The ball handler can start anywhere on the perimeter, and the screen can also come from different positions.
- Add defenders and build up to two-on-two.

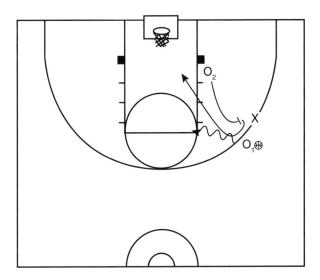

SLIP SCREEN

Gordy Presnell ┃ *Boise State University*

Purpose

To create a pressure release when the opponent double-teams or hedges out early on the pick-and-roll.

Organization

Use two offensive and two defensive players and one ball.

Procedure

1. The players set above the key in a two-guard front set.
2. Player O_2 begins to set an offense screen on defender X_1. Another defender hedges out to stop player O_1.
3. Player O_1 sees the second defender hedge and gives O_2 the backdoor cut sign, a closed fist.
4. Player O_2, seeing the fist, immediately dive-cuts toward the basket, receiving the pass from O_1.

Coaching Points

- Player O_2 must sell the screen before effectively slipping it.
- Player O_1 must read the defense and be prepared for a quick-hitting pass to O_2.

Variation

Defenders modify their positions so that O_1 and O_2 can read the defense and cut accordingly.

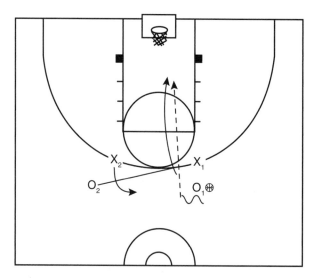

BACK SCREEN ROLL

Gordy Presnell | *Boise State University*

Purpose
To motivate the screener to be more offensively minded.

Organization
Use three players and one ball. The coach acts as a passer on the wing.

Procedure
1. Player O_2 begins on the weak side. Player O_1 initiates the drill from the top of the key.
2. Player O_1 passes to the coach, and O_2 sets a back screen on O_1's defender.
3. Player O_1 fades off the screen, preparing for a skip pass from the coach.
4. Player O_2 rolls to the ball.
5. The coach passes to O_1 or O_2 for a shot attempt.

Coaching Points
- Player O_2's back screen position on the defender should be diagonal.
- The screener's feet should be shoulder-width apart. Her arms should be crossed and her body balanced.
- Player O_2 should explode off the screen, rolling to the ball; her hands should be up and ready to receive the pass.

Variations
- Add two defenders on O_1 and O_2.
- Pick different spots on the floor to run the screen-and-roll depending on which offense is run.

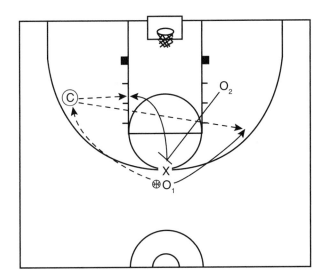

STAGGERED SCREEN

Gordy Presnell | *Boise State University*

Purpose

To develop proper technique for making a high cut, setting a pick-the-picker screen, making a flare cut, and rolling to the ball.

Organization

Use three players, one coach, and one ball. The players are positioned in a two-guard front with a wing. The coach occupies the other wing.

Procedure

1. Player O_1 initiates the drill by making a chest pass to the coach on the right wing.
2. Players O_2 and O_1 then move down and to the left to set a double staggered screen on O_3, who is cutting high (see figure 1).
3. Player O_2 turns and sets a pick-the-picker screen on O_1, who flares to the weakside wing.
4. Player O_2 rolls to the ball (see figure 2).
5. A coach may pass to any one of the three cutters.

Coaching Points

- Player O_3 must jab-step baseline to set up her defender. She drives off each screen shoulder to shoulder.
- Player O_1 makes a flare cut, then quickly backpedals to get in position for a skip pass from the coach.
- Player O_2 sets the screens and then immediately rolls to the strong side looking for the pass.

Variation

Add defenders, initially using one to try to break down the pick-the-picker flare cut. Then add two and three for a full live drill.

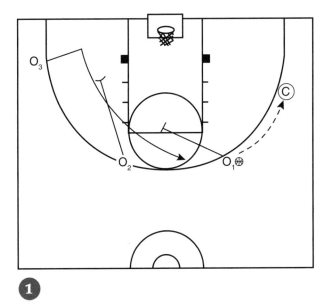

1

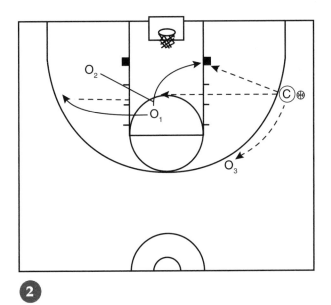

2

TRIANGLE DOWN SCREEN

Gordy Presnell | Boise State University

Purpose

To develop proper screening technique and post sealing and pinning while reading the defense.

Organization

Use three players and one ball.

Procedure

1. Players set up with a guard (O_1) at the wing with the ball. Player O_2 should be at the block and player O_3 at the elbow.
2. Player O_3 walks down and sets a screen on O_2's imaginary defender.
3. Player O_2 waits for the screen and goes high to the elbow.
4. Player O_3 posts up.
5. Player O_1 passes to O_2, and O_3 reverse seals and pins her imaginary defender.
6. The pass may go inside to O_3 on a pin.

Coaching Points

- The screener should have her arms crossed, her feet shoulder-width apart, and her knees slightly bent, and she should be balanced.
- As defense is added, O_1 may dribble baseline to create a better passing angle.

Variation

Add defenders and walk through the drill two times with live action and then rotate.

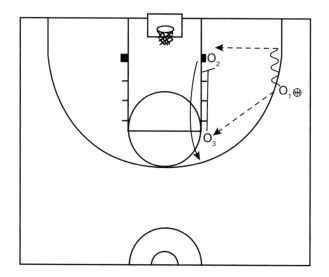

PIN AND SPIN

Wendy Larry | *Old Dominion University*

Purpose
To work on pinning, spinning, and sealing the defense after a switch has been made on a screen.

Organization
Use two passers, each with a ball: one at the top of the key and the other in a wing position. Two offensive players are on the blocks with coaches or managers for defense.

Procedure
1. Player O_1 sets a block-to-block screen for player O_2.
2. Player O_2 comes off the screen high or low.
3. The defense switches.
4. The first passer passes to O_2, who attempts to score.
5. The second passer passes to O_1, who has sealed her defender and has the defender pinned on her back. Player O_1 attempts to score.

Coaching Points
- Player O_1 must set a low, solid screen, and O_2 must set herself up by stepping away from the screen and then rubbing off the shoulder of her screener.
- The screener must use her arms legally to pin and then spin to the ball, showing a high target hand.

Variation
To help cutters get used to finishing with contact, managers use football blocking pads to bump the cutters as they attempt to score.

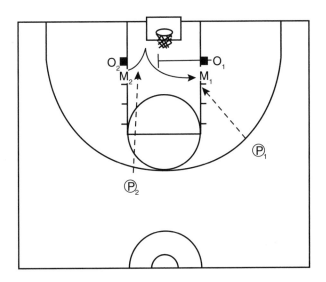

64 POST CROSS SCREENS: FLASH HIGH OR LOW

Charlene Thomas-Swinson | *University of Tulsa*

Purpose

To teach players how to set screens, use screens to get open, and read their teammates.

Organization

Use two balls and four players.

Procedure

1. Players O_1 and O_2 set up in the low post. P_1 and P_2 are passers. P_2 and a coach each have a ball at the top of the key.
2. The coach passes the ball to P_1 as O_1 sets a cross screen for O_2 by calling her name and setting the screen midline (see figure 1).
3. Player O_2 is slow to set up her defender and rubs shoulder to shoulder with O_1, then becomes quick in using the screen to get open (see figure 2).
4. Player O_1 reads where O_2 goes. If O_2 goes low to block, then O_1 flashes high to the foul line or elbow for a shot.
5. If O_2 goes high to the foul line, then O_1 flashes back to the ball block for a shot (see figure 3).
6. Remind P_2 that they always pass to the player on the block, and P_1 always passes to the player flashing to the elbow.

Coaching Points

- Teach players proper technique and body position for setting a screen as well as for using it.
- Talk to players about how to utilize a change of speed to get open off of a screen.
- Players should use proper body positioning when coming off a screen, and they should be ready to score.
- Make sure players communicate with teammates, and are aware when a screen is for them.

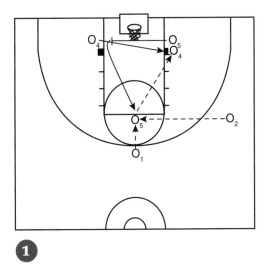

1

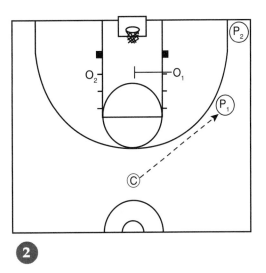

2

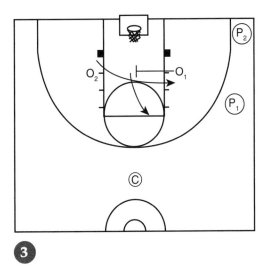

3

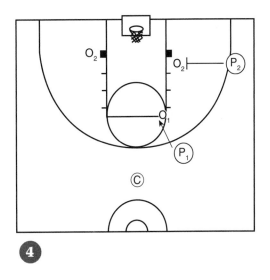

4

OFF-BALL SCREEN

Wendy Larry | *Old Dominion University*

Purpose

To develop the fundamentals of setting a screen, using a screen, and communicating between the screener and cutter.

Organization

Two passers are at the top of the key, each on a lane line extended; one has a ball. An offensive player is in the wing, one is on the block, and one manager as defense is on a block.

Procedure

1. Player O_1 sets a down screen for player O_2.
2. Player O_2 steps to the ball to set up her defense then rubs shoulders with the screener as she cuts off the screen.
3. The defense either fights over the screen or follows her player under the screen.
4. The screener (O_1) communicates with her teammate about what the defense chooses to do.
5. If the defense fights over, O_2 flares off the screen (see figure 1). If the defense trails, O_2 curls (see figure 2).
6. Player O_2 always steps to the ball after setting her screen.
7. The second passer always passes to the cutter closest to the basket while the first passer passes to the other player. Both players score.

Coaching Points

- Emphasize loud, precise communication. Players should call for the ball not only on a screen but also on a cut.
- Make sure O_1 is stationary and holds the screen long enough for O_2 to come off of it.
- The defense should be dummy—that is, just hold their positions—but if O_2 does not use the screen effectively, allow the defense to deny or steal the ball.

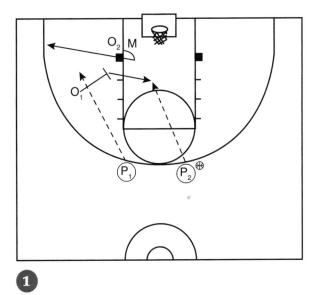

1

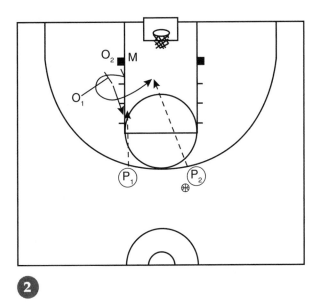

2

chapter 7

Shooting Drills

Great shooters—are they born or made? Whatever your opinion, there is no doubt that you will have your players' attention when you work on shooting. The feel and sound of a swish is motivation enough for most players to consider how they might improve their shooting fundamentals. And although not all shooters will have the touch of Diana Taurasi or the range of Katie Smith, you can still focus on the work ethic and repetition that all great shooters have in common.

So what will you teach your team about shooting that they do not think they already know? Perhaps you believe that shooters are born, so you will scan the grade schools and middle schools and seek talented recruits. Or better yet, you will read the following drills to see which new ideas you might incorporate into your skill development plan.

Teaching players how to refine their shots and modify their sometimes counterproductive idiosyncrasies in shooting is a challenge. Assume that all shooters—even if they are born with the skills—will benefit from your guidance and development. When players put in the extra hours and go the extra mile to gain their rhythm or correct a problem, you will see the results at game time.

OLYMPIC SHOOTING

Tara VanDerveer | Stanford University

Purpose

To practice two varieties of game shots off the move.

Organization

Use three players and two balls; shoot for 30 to 45 seconds and keep score. This drill can be competitive among groups.

Procedure

1. Start with one shooter (O_1) on the perimeter with a ball.
2. Player O_2 starts under the basket with a ball.
3. Player O_3 spots up ready to receive the ball from the player under the basket.
4. The shooter gets her own rebound and passes to an open player; after passing, the player spots up for a shot; relocate on every shot.

Coaching Points

- Players should stay within their shooting range but shoot from different spots.
- Players should be ready to shoot.
- Players must give a target and make sharp passes.

Variation

The shooter may take three-pointers, pull-ups, or a combination of shots.

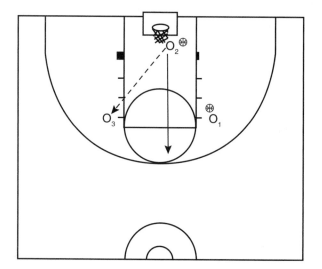

TICKTOCK SHOOTING

Tara VanDerveer | *Stanford University*

Purpose

To improve shooting consistency when taking shots at game tempo.

Organization

Everyone gets a partner, and each player has a ball; a coach or manager is a passer. Five minutes are on the clock.

Procedure

1. Each twosome starts at one of five shooting spots on the floor and makes a designated number of shots before moving on to the next spot.
2. If both shooters are taking three-pointers, the combined goal for shots made by the two players from each spot is 10.
3. If both shooters are taking two-pointers, the goal for shots made from each spot is 12.
4. If one shooter is taking three-pointers and the other two-pointers, the goal for shots made from each spot is 11.
5. The goal is for every twosome to finish the shots at all five spots before the clock runs out.

Coaching Points

- Players must take shots in their range.
- Players must be ready to shoot and must give a target for receiving the pass.

Variation

Add time and increase the number of shots for a greater challenge and to increase conditioning.

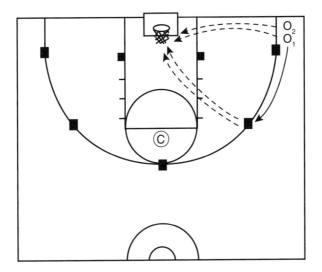

SHOOTING 100

Tara VanDerveer | *Stanford University*

Purpose

To improve shooting consistency and taking shots at game tempo with time pressure.

Organization

Everyone has a partner; a coach or manager is a passer. Put 12 minutes on the clock. Use five spots and two balls.

Procedure

1. The first player shoots 20 shots from the first spot, and the second player rebounds.
2. The second player shoots 20 from the same spot.
3. Pairs alternate shooters until both have taken 20 shots at five spots—100 shots per shooter.

Coaching Points

- Players must shoot at game pace to take the allotted number of shots in 12 minutes.
- Players must take shots in their range.
- Players must be ready to shoot and must give a target.
- Players must give sharp passes.

Variation

Add more time and increase the number of shots for a greater challenge and to increase conditioning.

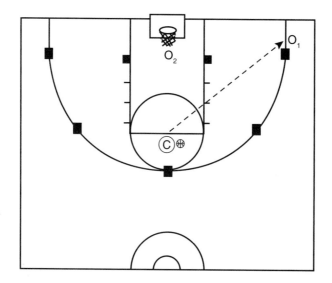

Mike Geary | *Michigan State University*

Purpose

To work on taking three-point shots, passing to teammates on the move, chasing long rebounds, and concentrating under pressure.

Organization

Use four lines of three players and two basketballs in each line.

Procedure

1. The player in the front of the line shoots a three-pointer from the wing and rebounds her shot.
2. The next player does the same.
3. The third player receives a pass from the first, shoots a three-point shot, and rebounds her shot.
4. The first player now receives a pass from the second.
5. The action continues for two minutes; on the whistle, all groups rotate clockwise to the next spot.
6. Players execute the drill for eight minutes.

Coaching Points

- Players must prepare to shoot by having their hands and feet ready.
- The passer calls the shooter's name when passing the ball.
- Players must sprint after the ball and when rotating lines.

Variations

- Keep players at each spot for one or three minutes.
- Place four players in each group and use three basketballs.

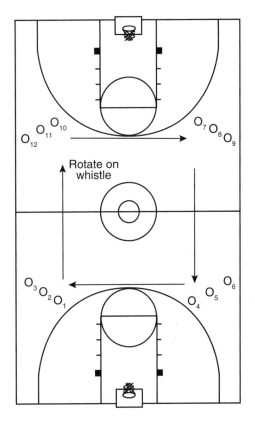

Mike Geary | *Michigan State University*

Purpose

To improve footwork and moving into shots, shooting shots off the catch, and shooting shots under pressure.

Organization

Use two players per basket and one ball.

Procedure

1. One player starts with the ball in one of the designated shooting spots (see figures 1-6).
2. The shooter shoots from this spot, then moves to the next while her partner rebounds and passes to her throughout the drill.
3. At the end of 55 seconds, the whistle sounds and the partners exchange positions.
4. Players have five seconds to complete the position exchange.
5. The whistle begins the next 55-second set.
6. A manager records the results.

Coaching Points

- The shooter should keep moving and time her cut so she gets to the spot at the same time as the pass.
- When the ball is in the air, the shooter should get her feet ready to receive the pass.
- The rebounder must work to help the shooter take as many shots as possible.

Variation

The passer passes with her weak hand.

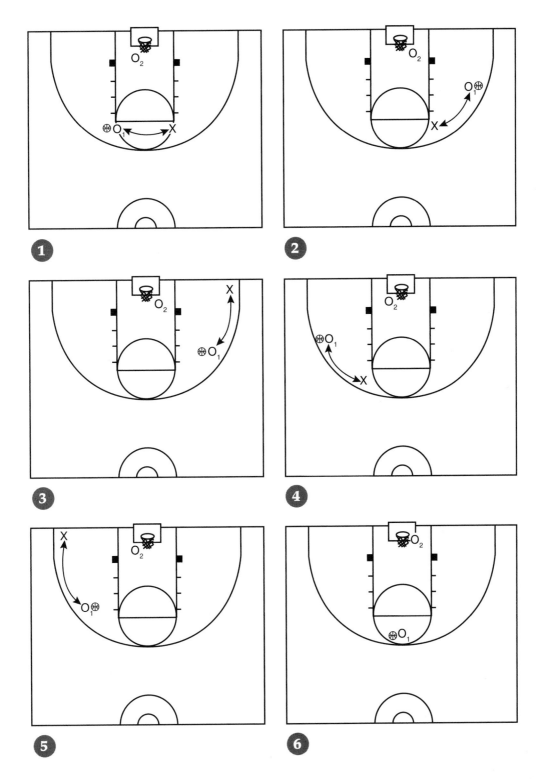

71   ZONE SHOOTING

Jon Newlee | Idaho State University

Purpose
To simulate game shots in certain areas on the floor where a zone defense may be vulnerable.

Organization
Three players fill the three guard spots. A coach with a ball starts at the top of the key, and coaches or managers fill the two wing spots at the free throw line extended. The first two post players start at the low blocks.

Procedure
1. The coach passes to one of the wings. The post players react on the pass. The strongside post pops out to the short corner (between the three-point line and the low block). The weakside post flashes in the middle toward the ball and ends up near the elbow of the key (see figure 1).
2. The wing makes a pass to either post player. From that point, the post player that received the pass has three options:
   - Catch and shoot
   - Catch and drive to the basket for a power layup (off of two feet) (see figures 2 and 3).
   - Catch, shot-fake, and make a bounce pass to the other post player who is cutting toward the strongside low block (see figures 4 and 5).
3. The posts rebound their own misses, put them back, and then the next two posts begin the drill.

Coaching Points
- Post players should make hard, decisive cuts.
- Players need to call for the ball and jump-catch when they receive it.
- Players should take game shots at game spots at game speed.

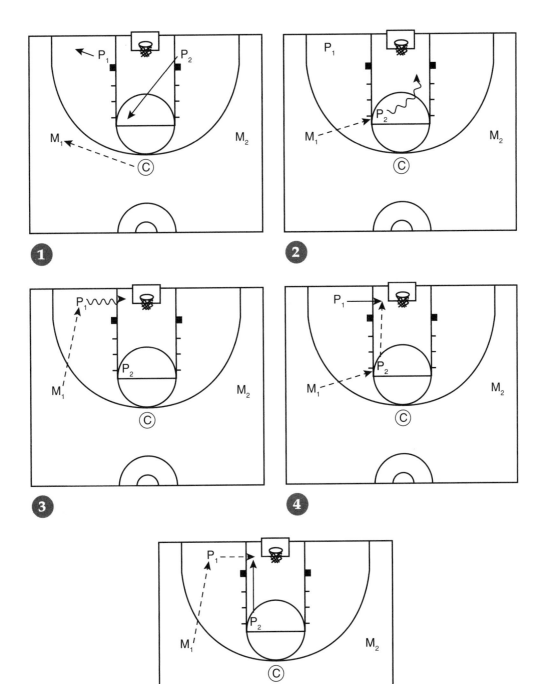

THIRTY-TWO

Mary Hegarty | *Long Beach State University*

Purpose

To improve three-point shots, jumpers, layups, and free throws by incorporating competition in the drill.

Organization

Mark five spots around the three-point line: at the right baseline, right wing, top of the key, left wing, and left baseline. The shooter is spotted at the left baseline. Her partner is under the basket with a ball.

Procedure

1. From each spot behind the three-point line, the shooter shoots a three-pointer, a one-dribble jump shot, and a layup.
2. Her partner rebounds and passes after each shot.
3. The three-pointer is worth 3, the jumper is worth 2, and the layup is worth 1. Six points are possible at each of the five spot, for a total of 30.
4. After shooting at all the spots, the shooter attempts two free throws, worth one point each. The series of shots has a potential score of 32 points.
5. Players should score in the mid- to high-20s. If they don't, they must perform a series of sprints determined by the coach.

Coaching Points

- The shooter should shoot at game speed.
- The shooter should call for the ball on each shot.
- Players should finish each shot before moving to next shot. They should not rush to the next shot.

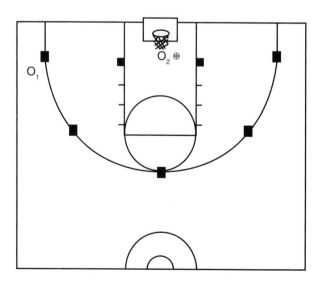

Variations

- Have the shooter start on the opposite baseline so she is moving in a different direction.
- Dictate which way the shooter goes on her one-dribble jump shot.
- Dictate which type of layup to take, for example, power, reverse.

73   BEAT LISA LESLIE

Mary Hegarty | Long Beach State University

Purpose
To challenge shooters to make more than 67 percent of their uncontested shots.

Organization
A passer with a ball is under the basket. The shooter is spotted on the perimeter 15 to 18 feet (4.6 to 5.5 meters) from the basket.

Procedure
1. The shooter begins to move around the perimeter, catching and shooting from various spots.
2. The passer rebounds all shots.
3. The shooter earns one point for every shot made. For every miss, Lisa Leslie gets two points.
4. Whoever gets 10 points first wins. For the shooter to win, she must make more than 67 percent of her shots.

Coaching Points
- The shooter should be low and ready to shoot when she receives a pass.
- The shooter should take all shots off of movement.
- When the ball is in the air, the shooter's feet should be in the air.
- The shooter should call for the ball on each pass.
- Passer should call out the score after each shot, announcing the shooter's score first.

Variations
- Have the player shoot one-dribble pull-ups.
- Increase the points for a miss or play the game to 20.
- Use the name of any good player or shooter instead of Lisa Leslie.
- If a player loses, have her run a series of sprints.

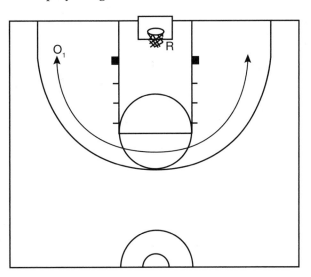

RAPID-FIRE SHOOTING

Mary Hegarty | Long Beach State University

Purpose

To improve the ability to make lots of shots in a short time and to improve passing skills and communication.

Organization

Three to six players form a line on the left wing, and three to six players form a line on the right wing. Each player has a ball except for the player at the front of one of the lines. She is the first shooter.

Procedure

1. Player O_1 receives a pass from the first player in the opposite line.
2. She catches the pass and shoots the ball, following her own shot. She goes to the end of the opposite line.
3. As soon as the pass has been made, the passer prepares to become the shooter and receive a pass from the player at the front of the opposite line.
4. The drill continues until the team has made a specified number of shots.

Coaching Points

- Players should call for the ball and be ready to receive the pass.
- While the ball is in the air, the player's feet should be in the air.
- The passer should make a sharp skip pass to the shooter.
- Players count made shots until the team reaches the goal.

Variations

- Line up the players anywhere, for example, both baselines, under the basket and at the top of the key.
- Have players start the drill by catching and shooting 15- to 18-foot (4.6- to 5.5-meter) shots. Add three-pointers, one-dribble pull-ups, and shots off movement.

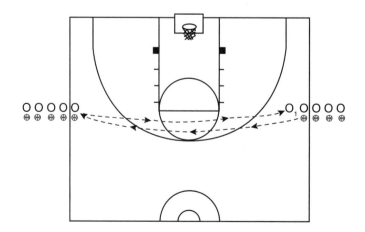

75   TRANSITION FINISHES

Mary Hegarty | *Long Beach State University*

Purpose

To improve the ability to finish a play in transition by practicing sliding and backpedaling and then shooting after sprinting. To improve conditioning and toughness.

Organization

A coach with the ball stands near the top of the key. Another coach or manager stands under the basket ready to rebound. Players stand in a line under the basket and off the baseline. This drill can be used for a few players or an entire team.

Procedure

1. The first player starts on the baseline under the basket with her back to half-court.
2. She begins by sliding along the baseline to the corner.
3. At the corner, she backpedals to the hash mark.
4. At the hash mark, she sprints and receives a pass from the coach at the top of key.
5. The next player in line begins after the player ahead of her hits the corner.
6. Once a player shoots on one side, she returns to the baseline and repeats the drill on the opposite side.
7. The drill continues until the group makes 15 shots.

Coaching Points

- Emphasize going hard and calling for the ball.
- On the sprint, have the shooters attack the basket at a 45-degree angle and use the glass on all shots.
- Encourage players to stay low on slides as they become fatigued.

Variations

- Change the goal for made shots depending on the size of the group and how challenging you want it to be.
- Have players shoot layups, jumpers, and one-dribble pull-ups. You can also add three-pointers.
- On the layups, hit the player with a pad to increase concentration and toughness.

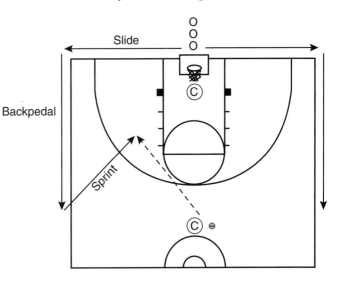

chapter 8

Offensive Rebounding Drills

Finding players who will attack the glass at both ends of the floor and control the boards will make a good coach a winning coach. Women's basketball has evolved from the days of tall and slow players dominating the boards. Now agile post players like Lisa Leslie, Lauren Jackson, and Cheryl Ford can run the floor, rip the boards, and score at the other end.

It's been said that rebounding and defense make the difference in winning programs. With bigger, stronger, and fitter players, rebounding requires a serious gut check for most, and smaller players like Alana Beard and Deanna Nolan get more than their share of rebounds by effort and anticipation. There is plenty of contact on the boards, too, but a hearty reward for those who battle well: a quick transition to the other end.

Help your players learn the basics of good offensive rebounding: seeing the angle of the shot, assuming every shot is missed, and pursuing until they have the ball. A little hard work and sweat—not to mention a few bruises—can turn an average player into an invaluable one on the boards.

David Smith | *Bellarmine University*

Purpose
To teach teams how to rebound off a missed free throw.

Organization
Use seven players, a coach or manager, one ball, and one basket.

Procedure
1. Station seven players around the free throw lane. The coach or manager shoots the free throws.
2. On the free throw attempt, the defensive players carry out their block-out assignments.
3. After each rebound, the defensive players rotate clockwise.
4. Once the defensive players have been at each position, switch the offensive and defensive players.

Coaching Points
- Emphasize quickness and making contact as soon as the ball is released or upon hitting the rim, depending on your rules.
- Emphasize using the proper block-out technique.
- Remind defensive players that when they know where the ball will end up after a missed shot, they should release and go get the ball.

Variation
Make this a contest. Award 2 points for an offensive rebound and 1 point for a defensive rebound. The first team to 10 points wins.

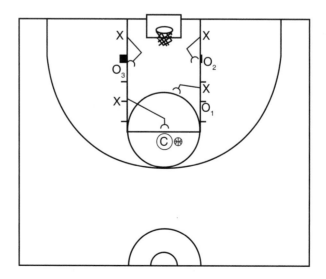

77 BACK ROLL

David Smith | *Bellarmine University*

Purpose
To teach offensive players to roll off a block-out to gain an offensive rebound.

Organization
Use any number of players, one coach or manager, one ball, and one basket.

Procedure
1. Position a defender in a block-out position facing the basket. Player O_1 is positioned on the rear of the player blocking out. The rest of the players form a line behind the free throw circle.
2. The coach or manager is off to the side of the lane with a basketball. The coach tosses the ball off the backboard so that it rebounds into the lane.
3. When the ball leaves the coach's hand, the offensive player rolls off the back of the defender (who is not giving resistance) and goes after the ball. The offensive player tries to catch the ball before it hits the floor.
4. Once the player has secured the rebound, she keeps the ball high, steps to the basket, and puts the ball in the basket. If she is more than one step from the basket, she takes a dribble.
5. The offensive player then becomes the defender, and the defender goes to the end of the line.

Coaching Points
- Have the offensive player do a 360-degree roll off the defender.
- Remind the offensive player to keep her hands up in front of her as she rolls because the ball will often hit her hands before she visually finds the ball.
- Move to each side of the lane so that players have a chance to roll in each direction. Some can roll one way but struggle going the other.

Variation
To teach offensive players to roll, station a single player at the free throw line. The player throws the ball off the board, does a 360-degree roll, catches the ball, and puts it back in the basket.

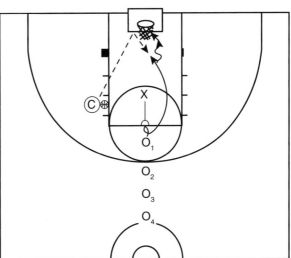

David Smith | Bellarmine University

Purpose

To teach players to find someone to block out, go to that player and make contact, find the ball, release, and then go get the ball.

Organization

Five players stand around the three-point circle. Two defenders are in the middle of the free throw lane, facing away from the basket. One coach is under the basket, and another coach or manager is on the perimeter with a basketball.

Procedure

1. The coach under the basket points at two offensive players on the perimeter, and the other coach or manager shoots the ball.
2. The two designated offensive players go for the rebound, and the defense locates the designated offensive players, moves to them, and blocks them out. The defender holds her block-out until she locates the ball, releases, and goes to get the rebound (see figure 1).
3. Once the rebound has been secured, either by the defense or offense, the ball is returned to the coach on the perimeter. The offensive players go back to their original positions, the defense returns to the middle of the lane, and the drill is repeated with the same or a different combination of offensive players being designated.

Coaching Points

- The initial defensive contact with the offensive players must be outside the lane.
- Players should focus on proper block-out technique.
- When the defensive player knows where the ball will end up after a missed shot, she must release and go get the ball.
- The defense must communicate who they will block out so that both don't go to the same offensive player.
- When the coach is satisfied with the efforts of the defense, players change positions with two of the offensive players on the perimeter.

Variation

If you are working with young players and just beginning to teach blocking out or you don't have someone to shoot the ball, make these adjustments to the drill:
- Have only one defender in the middle and place the ball on the floor behind the defense (see figure 2).
- Designate only one offensive player to go for the ball and be blocked out.
- After designating the offensive player, blow the whistle for the drill to begin.
- Have the defense hold the block-out until the whistle is blown (three to five seconds after the initial contact).
- Reduce the number of players on the perimeter to three or four.

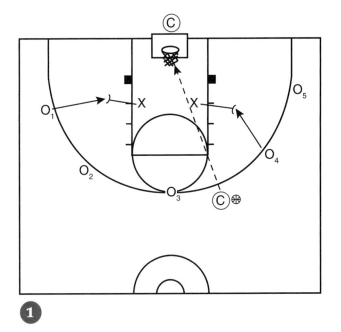

1

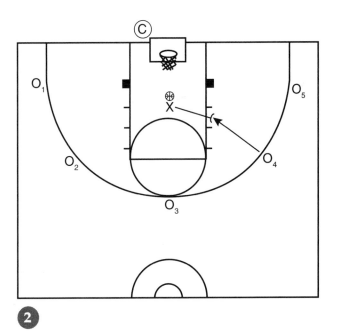

2

Debbie Ryan | *University of Virginia*

Purpose

To learn how to rebound out of live player-to-player situations.

Organization

Five offensive players start on the baseline, five defensive players are at half-court facing them, and two coaches are positioned in the far corners of the court near the baseline.

Procedure

1. The five offensive players weave to half-court, passing the ball to the middle player at half-court (see figure 1).
2. The middle player passes the ball to the end player on one side or the other. The end player then passes the ball to one of the coaches on the baseline.
3. The players at half-court try to offensively rebound the ball. They may run anywhere on the court (see figure 2).
4. The defense has to react and pick up the open players and communicate with their teammates so that all the offensive players are covered.
5. When the coach receives the ball, she shoots immediately, and both teams try to rebound the ball (see figure 3).

Coaching Points

- As the five-person weave occurs, the defense works on communicating and matching up as the ball is passed.
- As the ball is passed, the defense moves into proper help positions.
- The defense should maintain a box-out and throw strong outlet passes when they rebound the ball.
- A scoring system helps to make the drill more competitive (e.g., one point for a defensive rebound, one point for an offensive rebound, and one point to score).

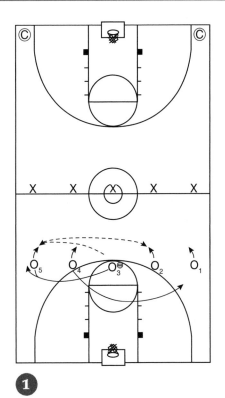

1

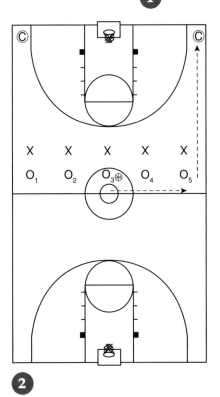

2

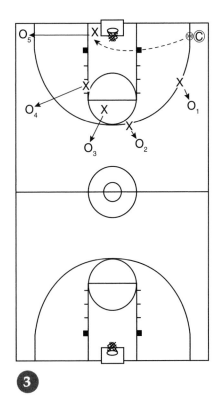

3

HIT AND REBOUND

Patrick Knapp | University of Pennsylvania

Purpose

To work on team reaction and reading angles on rebounds.

Organization

Use four or more players in two lines, one ball, and one coach.

Procedure

1. Line up pairs of players at either elbow—two offensive and two defensive.
2. The coach has the ball in the key area. The defense is in a defensive stance, and the offense is in a ready position.
3. The coach yells "go," and the defense hits the deck and does a quick push-up.
4. The coach shoots the ball as the defense stands up. The defense adjusts, uses box-out footwork, makes contact, sees the rim, and gets the ball. The offense should attack the rim on the shot, look to knife off the shoulder of the block-out player or hit one side of their body, spin off the block-out player, try to hook the elbow of the block-out player for leverage, and beat defense to the ball.
5. The offense becomes the defense, and the defense goes off.

Coaching Points

- Timing the shot is key.
- Players must react and hustle.
- Holding is not allowed. Players must use proper box-out footwork.

Variation

Don't let the defense off until they get one or more rebounds. The offense must attack the basket with fakes and spins.

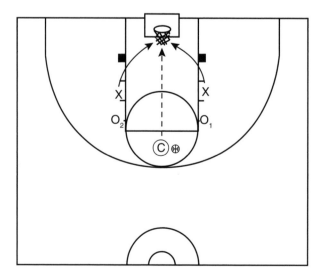

81   TWO-BALL REBOUNDING

Patrick Knapp | University of Pennsylvania

Purpose

To teach players to use extra effort when rebounding offensively and to box out, rebound, and outlet the ball.

Organization

Use three offensive players and three defensive players, two coaches or managers, and two balls.

Procedure

1. The drill involves three-on-three competition between the offense and defense.
2. Start the drill with the coach or manager shooting the ball.
3. If the defense gains control, they should outlet to a coach or manager.
4. If the offense gains control, they should try to score.
5. As soon as the first ball is controlled, the coach or manager shoots a second ball.
6. Both groups rebound both shots. Continue the drill until the offense rebounds and scores.

Coaching Points

- The defense should always make contact and move to the ball.
- The offense should go after the rebounds aggressively. The offense stops, cuts, and spins to get into position.

Variation

Players screen, move, and cut using three-on-three motion concepts in order to change the defense's position.

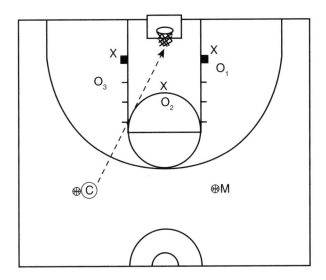

TWO-ON-TWO, WEAKSIDE REBOUNDING

Patrick Knapp | *University of Pennsylvania*

Purpose

To work on defending and boxing out against a screen-and-cut offense.

Organization

An offensive player is at the baseline, and another one is at the wing. A defensive player is at the baseline, and another one is at the wing. Two coaches or managers are at the top of the circle on opposite sides. Use one ball.

Procedure

1. Line up in a two-on-two, weakside down screen position.
2. The coach is opposite the guard and the wing.
3. The ball starts in the offensive guard's hands. She passes to the coach.
4. After the pass, the players go into a down screen movement (see figure 1).
5. Proper offensive and defensive screening rules apply.
6. The coach shoots the ball or passes to the manager, who shoots from the corner (see figure 2).

Coaching Points

- The defense should talk, see the ball, and play the help side.
- The defense should make contact and force the offense one way and pivot the other.
- The offense should cut and spin to the hoop and rebound aggressively.

Variations

- Play live. If you or a manager see an open player, pass to her.
- Switch after three possessions, or the defense can stay on until they stop or rebound.
- Assign the defense sprints or push-ups for every offensive rebound.
- Teach offensive rebounding steps, cuts, and spins.

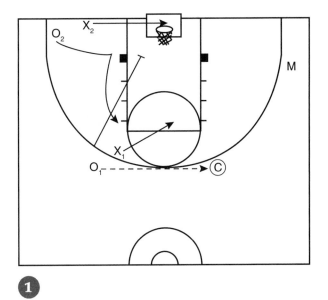

1

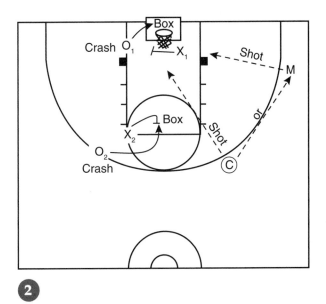

2

FIGURE-8 REBOUNDING

Patrick Knapp | *University of Pennsylvania*

Purpose

To teach players ball control while tipping and rebounding and to improve conditioning.

Organization

Three players stand at a basket with one ball.

Procedure

1. The ball starts on the two-player side of the rim.
2. Player O_2 tosses the ball at an angle against the backboard to create a rebound for player O_3.
3. As this is done, O_2 runs behind O_3.
4. The coach designates a certain number of tips in a row (e.g., 20) or tipping for a certain amount of time (e.g., 45 seconds). The last player finishes with a basket.

Coaching Points

- Younger players may catch the ball with two hands and come down, chin the ball, and go back up. More experienced players can tip with one or two hands and keep the ball moving.
- When tipping, players must keep the ball high.
- Players should rebound the ball with two hands at the peak of the jump.
- Players should focus on maintaining balance and control.
- Players should use proper two-hand and two-foot techniques.
- Players should attack the ball and move constantly.

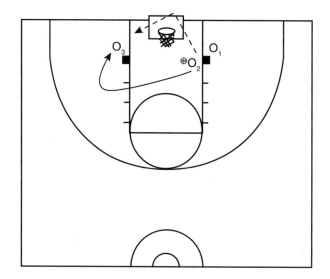

THREE-LINE REBOUNDING

Theresa Grentz | *University of Illinois*

Purpose

To teach multiple efforts in securing rebounds.

Organization

Three lines of players are at the three-point circle: one line at each wing and one line at the top of the key. The first person in each line is the defender; the second person is the offensive player. The coach has the ball and begins anywhere on the court she or he desires.

Procedure

1. The defense begins the drill by slapping the floor from a defensive stance and yelling "defense."
2. The coach shoots and intentionally misses a shot.
3. The offensive players attempt to rebound, and the defensive players box out first and then rebound.
4. If the offense rebounds, the offensive player puts the ball back up immediately from the location of the rebound.
5. If the defense rebounds, the defender outlets the basketball to the person in the closest wing position, and that person dribbles the full length of the court and scores the layup.
6. While the ball is in transition to the other end, the defense steps off and the offense becomes the defense; a new offense steps up.
7. The coach is ready for another missed shot.
8. The drill is continuous: changing the defense and offense should occur quickly.

Coaching Points

- This drill teaches the offense to make multiple attempts to gain a rebound, and it teaches the defense to hold their box-out position until their team can secure the rebound.
- Players should maintain their intensity and focus on completing the task. The transition is important and should be emphasized.

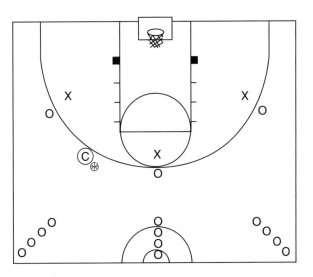

Theresa Grentz | *University of Illinois*

Purpose

To work on shell defense positioning, boxing out and rebounding, transition, execution, and transition defense.

Organization

Use two teams (team A has four players, and team B has three), one ball, and one coach.

Procedure

1. The coach has the ball.
2. Team B passes and moves, keeping the floor spread and forcing team A to play defense.
3. Only the coach can shoot the ball (coaches can decide if the offense can score another way, such as only off a layup).
4. Once the coach shoots, team A boxes out and rebounds the ball (if the shot is made, team A takes the ball out of bounds).
5. Team A outlets the ball and transitions down to the other end with team B now on defense (a four-on-three situation; see figure 1).
6. Team A works on scoring when they have a numerical advantage (see figure 2).
7. On the shot, team B boxes out and rebounds and outlets the ball and transitions back to the original end of the court. Team A is again on defense (see figure 3).
8. Team B works on scoring when they have a numerical disadvantage (see figure 4).
9. When a team scores, the coach stops play and resets the drill.
10. A new team comes on, or team A starts on offense and team B starts on defense.

Coaching Points

- Emphasize boxing out and rebounding.
- Work on transition offense with a numerical advantage.
- Work on transition defense with a numerical disadvantage.

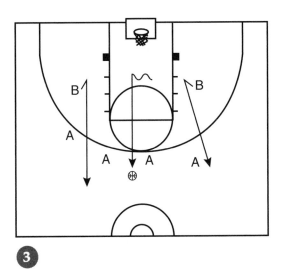

1

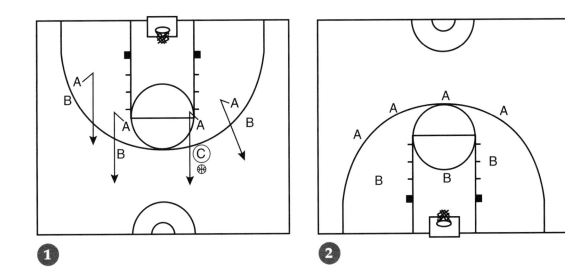

2

3

4

COMPETITIVE REBOUNDING

Nancy Fahey | Washington University

Purpose

To help reinforce rebounding position in a two-on-two competitive situation.

Organization

Players form lines on either side of the lane. Defenders are under the basket. The offense is in two lines at the elbows.

Procedure

1. Team A plays team B two-on-two with no dribbling.
2. Team A passes the ball to team B. Team B shoots off the pass.
3. Team A follows the pass, defends the shot, and boxes out.
4. If the shot is made, quickly reset the drill.
5. Team B crashes the offensive boards.
6. The team that gets the rebound tries to score. Players may dribble during this part of the drill. The team that scores goes to the elbows and the drill continues.
7. Run the drill for three to five minutes. When the time is up, the team under the basket has a consequence, such as running sprints.

Coaching Points

- Watch for excessive fouling. However, this drill is physical.
- Keep the drill moving and switch players so that they go against different competitors from time to time.

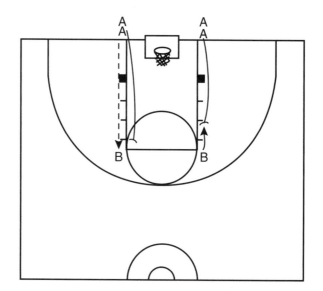

87 CIRCLE BOX-OUT

Nancy Fahey | Washington University

Purpose
To help simulate zone rebounding responsibilities.

Organization
Use three stationary offensive players, three moving defensive players, one coach, and one ball.

Procedure
1. On a signal from the coach, the defense rotates positions clockwise. Every time they move, they must call out the name of the person they are guarding.
2. The coach shoots the ball when the defensive players are between the offensive players and the basket.
3. The defense must communicate with each other and box out all three offensive players.

Coaching Points
- The defense may not double-team offensive players.
- The offense should crash the boards.
- All defensive players should move while in their defensive stance.

Variation
As the defensive players circle clockwise, the coach yells "switch." The defense changes directions and rotates counterclockwise. Again, the coach shoots the ball when the defense is between the offensive players and the basket.

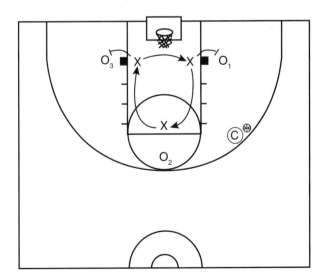

Nancy Fahey | *Washington University*

Purpose

To reinforce backside rebounding responsibilities (can be used as a warm-up).

Organization

Players form three lines at half-court.

Procedure

1. Player O_1 passes to O_2, who dribbles hard to the free throw line as O_1 circles behind her. Player O_3 sprints to the middle of the lane in a defensive position (see figure 1).
2. Player O_2 passes back to O_1, who is now at the wing, then reverses to the opposite wing area.
3. Player O_1 executes a front crossover dribble to the baseline and pulls up for a jumper (see figure 2).
4. Player O_3 must turn and box out O_2 who is acting as a weakside rebounder. O_3 should box her outside of the lane line.
5. The drill repeats with three different players.

Coaching Points

- The defensive player's first look on the shot is to box out O_2. She must step toward O_2, not toward the basket.
- Most rebounds come off the opposite side of the basket from the shot; therefore, it is important that the weakside rebounder have a good angle to rebound the basketball.

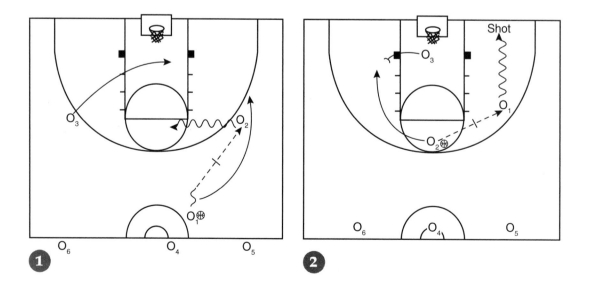

89

BOX OUT AND GO

Jody Conradt I *University of Texas*

Purpose

To improve boxing out and making the outlet pass to start an offensive transition.

Organization

The coach or manager is the shooter at the free throw line. An offensive and a defensive player match up on either side of the lane about midway down. Players should form outlet lines on either side of the floor.

Procedure

1. When the shot goes up, each defender boxes out her player and secures the rebound (see figure 1).
2. The ball should be passed to the nearest side outlet player.
3. The two outlet players take the ball two on one (versus the rebounder) to the other end of the floor and convert (see figure 2).

Coaching Points

- The offense rotates to become the defense.
- The next two players in each outlet line become offensive players.

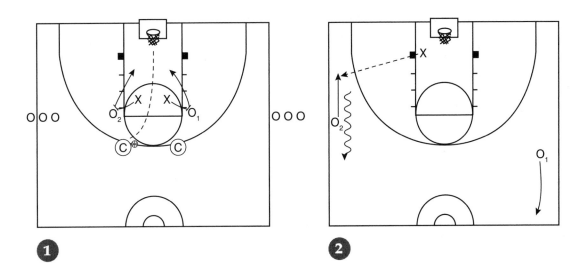

chapter 9

Offensive Transition Drills

Transition basketball comes in many packages. Whether your team has speed and savvy, disciplined precision, or a wide-open attack, the goal remains the same: to score at the other end when they have an advantage.

Without a doubt, transition offense is the closest thing to playground ball; however, skills, discipline, and creativity all must blend into the team philosophy, which accounts for the many looks of the transition game. Some teams attack fast and furiously; others alternate their pace to catch their defenders off guard. Some shoot quickly and from long range, and others only attempt layups. Whatever your team's style, putting your plan into action involves a lot of preliminary steps. Who will handle the ball? Will the ball come up the sideline or the middle? Will the team dribble the ball or pass it? Who is your primary attacker off a drive or a pull-up? Answer these questions first, then read on into the following drills and put your plan into action.

BREAK ON NUMBERS

Muffet McGraw | *University of Notre Dame*

Purpose

To work on the following skills after a quick score: looking up, throwing the ball ahead, making good decisions, and finding the open player.

Organization

Use 9 or 10 players: 5 on offense in the lane at one end of the court and everyone else at half-court out of bounds. Use two coaches and one ball.

Procedure

1. The coach misses a shot, and the offense rebounds, outlets, and fills the lane.
2. Another coach is at half-court and sends out one to five defenders.
3. The offense must find the open player and try to score quickly.
4. When the play is over, the offense stays in the lane and the defense returns to half-court; the coach shoots, and the drill is repeated.

Coaching Points

- Everyone rebounds; they may run a pattern, break, or just fill the lanes.
- Players should turn to the outside for an outlet pass; the point guard calls for the ball.
- Players should run hard and run wide on the wings.

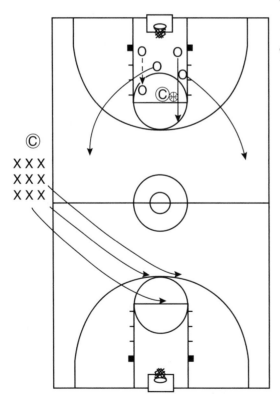

Variation

Send more defenders (up to five) to catch up to the ball. In other words, send two more defenders to turn a 5 on 3 into a 5 on 5 situation if the offense is making too many passes or isn't scoring quickly enough.

CELTICS FAST BREAK

Barbara Stevens | *Bentley College*

Purpose

To improve the execution of full-court layups and the baseball outlet pass and to improve conditioning.

Organization

Players split into two groups: one group under the basket and the other in an outlet line on the sideline at the free throw line extended. Use two or three balls.

Procedure

1. The first player under the basket steps out, tosses the ball off the board, and throws an outlet pass to the first player in the outlet line.
2. The outlet player speed dribbles down the court and takes a layup. The rebounder sprints to follow the shot and puts back any misses.
3. The rebounder then takes a made shot out of bounds and throws a baseball pass to the first player, who is sprinting down the sideline. This player speed dribbles and takes the layup.
4. The next rebounder waiting takes the ball out of the net, outlets to the next player in the outlet line, and they perform the drill.
5. This is a continuous drill; the new group can begin when the first layup is taken at the opposite end of the floor.

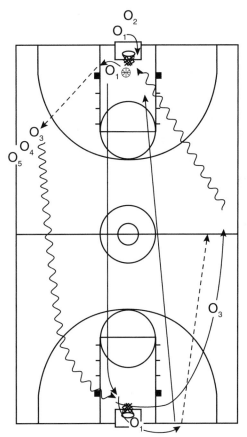

Coaching Points

- Players must call for the outlet pass.
- Players must execute accurate overhead outlet passes.
- Players should throw the baseball pass over the receiver's inside shoulder.

Variations

- Run this drill on both sides of the floor.
- Run the drill for a designated amount of time or until a certain number of layups is reached.
- Keep players in the same lines or have them change lines.
- Have the shooter pull up for a jumper or a three-pointer.

Barbara Stevens | *Bentley College*

Purpose

To teach recognition of filling lanes on a fast break. This drill stresses communication and is a great conditioner.

Organization

Use one ball and five players: a rebounder, an outlet, a middle, a left wing, and a right wing. All players are positioned below the top of the three-point circle extended.

Procedure

1. The rebounder starts the drill by tossing the ball off the backboard. The other players break to the outlet, middle, right wing, and left wing.
2. The rebounder throws the ball to the outlet, who passes to the middle. As the rebounder passes, the wings sprint down the court. The middle passes to the left wing, and the left wing passes to the right wing, who cuts in for the layup (see figure 1).
3. Players change positions by calling out their positions, and they repeat the drill back down the court.
4. Players should not dribble the ball, and the ball must not touch the floor until the final pass, which can be a bounce pass. It takes four passes to score. Run this drill down and back twice (see figure 2).

Coaching Points

- Players must call out their positions and learn to see what lanes are filled; they must then sprint to the open lane.
- Players must call out their positions to alert the passer of the next pass, for example, outlet, middle, left, right, or rebound.

Variation

To improve conditioning, run it several more times.

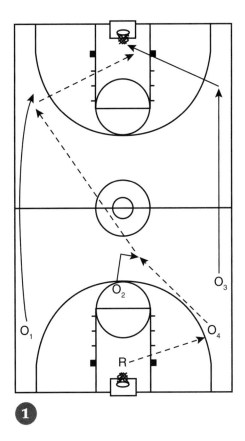

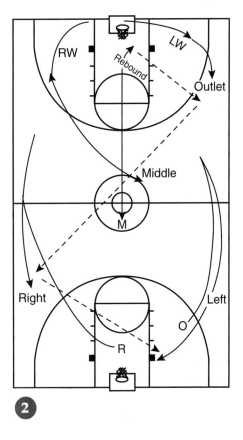

1

2

THREE-ON-TWO, TWO-ON-ONE CONTINUOUS CONVERSION

Barbara Stevens | Bentley College

Purpose

To teach offensive and defensive decision making in numerical advantage and disadvantage situations.

Organization

Three players begin the drill on the end line with the ball in the middle. Two tandem defenders start in the center circle. The rest of the team is split into two outlet lines at one end of the court.

Procedure

1. The three offensive players attack the two defenders.
2. If the offense scores or the defense gets possession, the two defenders come back on offense against the last player to touch the ball on offense for a two on one (see figure 1).
3. The two remaining, formerly offensive, players go to the center-court circle to become the next tandem defenders (see figure 2).
4. Players take only one shot in the two-on-one segment. Whether it's made or missed, any of the three players may outlet the ball to one of the outlet lines and fill a lane in the next group of three to attack the waiting tandem defense.

Coaching Points

- The coach limits the number of passes the offense makes to score. The more passes made, the more time the defenders have to recover.
- Players should pass the ball ahead to shift the defense.
- Defenders need to talk and shift quickly in an effort to force the offense into several passes.

Variation

Run this drill for a designated amount of time. It is competitive and can reward the player who hustles to stay in the drill.

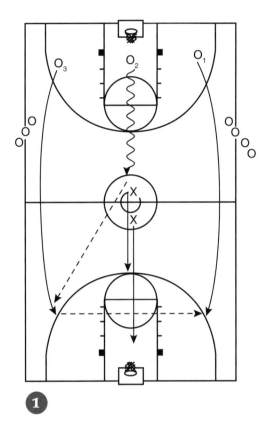

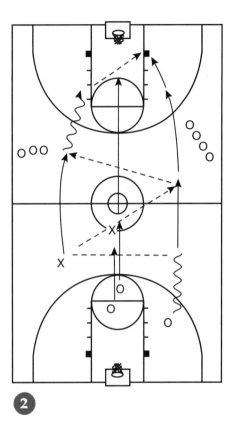

1

2

AIR IT OUT

Theresa Grentz | *University of Illinois*

Purpose

To teach transition passing, catching, and shooting and to improve conditioning.

Organization

Divide the team into two equal groups. One group is under the basket outside the free throw lane, and the second group is out of bounds in the wing area along the sideline. Use two balls.

Procedure

1. The first person in the baseline group (O₁) tosses the ball off the backboard, rebounds it, and passes it to the first person in the sideline group.
2. The first person in the sideline group (O₂) steps onto the court to assume the wing position as the ball is being tossed off the backboard.
3. Player O₂ receives the outlet, dribbles the length of the court, and executes a layup. The original rebounder (O₁) follows the play, rebounds the made layup, and takes the ball out of bounds.

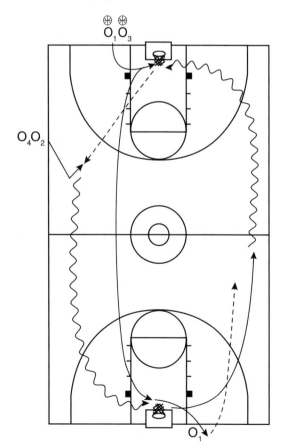

4. Player O₂, after making the layup, breaks to the opposite wing and runs long and wide down the sideline.
5. Player O₂ receives the pass from O₁ and executes a layup. Player O₁ follows the play to rebound the shot.
6. The ball is passed to the next person in the baseline group and players O₁ and O₂ switch lines.
7. The next pair of players begin their turn when the first layup is made at the opposite end of the court.

Coaching Points

- Emphasize proper technique when releasing the pass and controlling the spin of the ball so players can throw a long pass with accuracy.
- To use the drill for conditioning, have players perform it for a minimum of two minutes on each side of the basket.

TRANSITION SHOOTING

Wes Moore | *University of Tennessee at Chattanooga*

Purpose

To simulate the game situation of a post trailing in transition and to practice options for scoring when the ball is reversed to her.

Organization

Post players each have a ball and form a line at midcourt. Two coaches serve as passers.

Procedure

1. The first player passes the ball to a coach and runs down the middle of the floor to the top of the key.
2. The coach passes the ball back to the player.
3. The player sweeps the ball through and attacks the basket for a layup opposite where the pass came from.
4. The player grabs her own rebound and dribbles around the outside of the court and returns to the line.
5. After everyone has gone twice, the first player passes to the other sideline and performs the layup on the other side.
6. Repeat the drill with players taking one hard dribble opposite and then pulling up for a jumper.
7. Repeat the drill with players catching and shooting a three-pointer. If a player is uncomfortable shooting a three-pointer, the passers should hit her near the foul line.

Coaching Points

- On the layup, the player should be low and strong when she sweeps and then push the dribble out in front to the hole. Footwork is important for preventing traveling.
- On the jumper, the player should sweep and go hard to get the defense on their heels. Players should maintain control and go straight up on the jump shot without drifting.
- On the catch-and-shoot, players should run to the spot and then gather themselves on the shot. Players can also use a jab step to sell the drive before taking the shot.

Variations

- A coach just below the top of the key contests the sweep and works on the offense driving tightly off the defense's shoulder.
- A coach plays dummy defense and makes the offense read and react with the correct move.

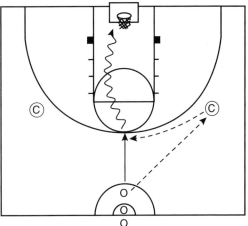

WEAVE SHOOTING

Bob Lindsay | *Kent State University*

Purpose

To develop full-speed passing and shooting in transition.

Organization

Use three lines of players on both baselines and four balls: one on the baseline where the drill starts and three on the opposite baseline.

Procedure

1. Three players weave from one baseline to the other.
2. The first shooter—the player who has the ball at the end of the weave—makes a layup, rebounds, and steps off the court.
3. The second and third players receive diagonal skip passes from baseline passers for 15-foot (4.6-meter) shots or three-pointers, rebound, and step off the court (see figure 1).
4. The next group starts a weave from the baseline and repeats the drill; the middle player starts the group (see figure 2).

Coaching Points

- Allow no turnovers and assess a penalty for missed shots.
- Set shooting percentage goals and a time limit.
- Remind players to run at full speed, stay wide, and communicate.

Variation

Shoot different shots.

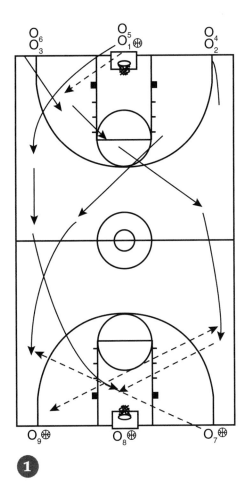

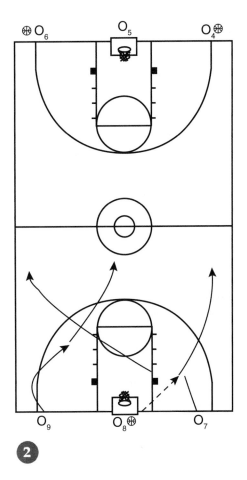

1

2

Kathy Delaney-Smith | *Harvard University*

Purpose

To teach transition principles, teamwork, and poise under pressure.

Organization

Use three teams of four players and one ball.

Procedure

1. Team A starts at half-court with the ball and goes four on two against team B.
2. The two players from team B who are at half-court outside the sideline step on the court and play defense as the ball crosses half-court to become four on four (see figure 1).
3. Team B rebounds a miss (or takes it out of bounds after a made shot) and goes four on two against team C, who has stepped on at the opposite end of the court (see figure 2).
4. Teams start with only two defending, and two more can enter the court once the ball passes half-court.

Coaching Points

- Players should remain poised in this fast-paced game.
- Players should look for a numerical advantage, then play controlled four on four.
- Winners don't have to run sprints at the end.

Variations

- Add defensive pressure before the ball crosses half-court and on the inbounds pass.
- Add a requirement (e.g., the offense must pass to the post player at least once).

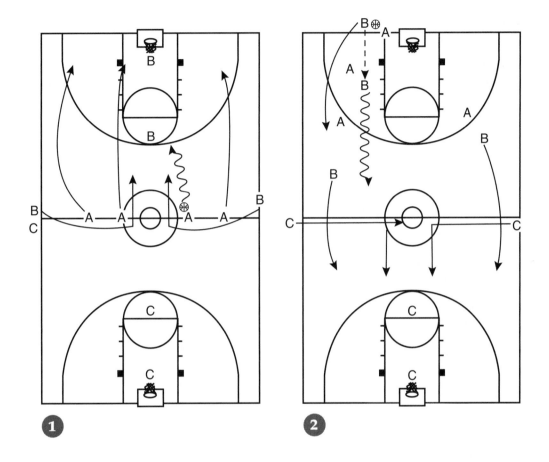

Bill Gibbons | *College of the Holy Cross*

Purpose

To work on securing loose balls and speed dribbling while not under pursuit.

Organization

One player stands downcourt at the free throw line; the others are in two lines on the baseline (one line is offensive and the other is defensive). The coach stands with one ball at the free throw line.

Procedure

1. The coach drops the ball. On the first whistle, player O_1 sprints to pick up the ball at the free throw line and speed dribbles down the court.
2. On the second whistle, player X_1 sprints to tap the ball away to her teammate X_2 (see figure 1).
3. Player X_2 is ready to secure a tapped ball, and she keeps her head up to avoid the offensive player running at her.
4. Player X_1 taps the ball away and then changes direction to look for a pass from X_2.
5. After receiving the pass, X_1 makes a strong layup, and X_2 sprints to get the rebound before it hits the floor.
6. Player X_2 outlets the ball to the coach and the next two in line go on the next whistles. Player O_1 remains at the downcourt free throw line to become the new X_2 (see figure 2).

Coaching Points

- Players should pick up loose balls with two hands and keep their heads up when speed dribbling downcourt.
- All players should sprint back through the play.
- Players should be ready to secure loose balls, avoid the opponent, and make good passes for an easy two points, then sprint to follow up.

Variation

Hit X_1 directly; she can fan out to the wing position (as if no one were going to the hoop) and wait to hit the trailer (X_2) with a chest pass for a jumper. Both players go to the boards hard and finish the play if the shot is missed. Players should change lines, work on dribbling with the other hand, and look to tap the ball away.

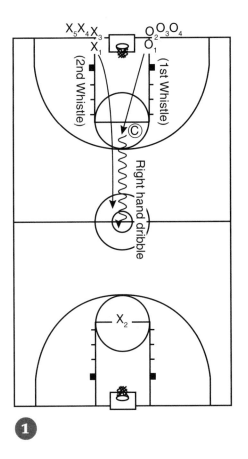

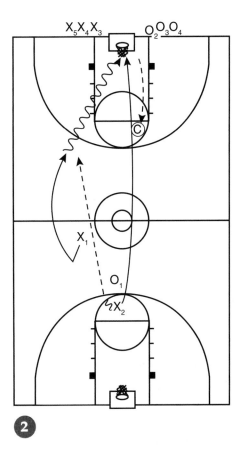

1

2

THREE-PLAYER BREAK

Joan Bonvicini | *University of Arizona*

Purpose

To teach players to fill all three lanes as quickly as possible. This drill gives players options to run in a three-player break situation.

Organization

The entire team lines up in three lines on the baseline. Each player in the center line has a ball.

Procedure

1. Players are in three lines at the baseline. Each group of three should have at least one post player.
2. The first three players step out, with player P under the basket and players W and G at the elbows of the key.
3. Player P tosses the ball off the backboard and rebounds yelling "ball." The other two players sprint to the sidelines calling "outlet." The rebounder makes an overhead pass to either player W or G and then fills the lane opposite her pass.
4. Player W sprints to the middle of the floor yelling "middle." The outlet (player G) now makes a chest pass to player W (see figure 1).
5. Player W dribbles up the court. Both wings are wide, calling their lanes either "right" or "left."
6. Player W jump-stops outside the key and bounce-passes to one of the wings for a layup. The other wing rebounds if the shot is missed (see figure 2).
7. Once the shot is made, the players step off, and the next three players in line begin the drill. The drill continues until all groups of three have shot a layup.
8. Once all groups have completed the drill, add options, such as the following:
   - A bounce pass for a layup
   - A jump shot from the wing with a rebounder putting up a shot if the wing misses
   - A pass back to the top where the middle player jump-stops at the top of the key and passes to the wing, who fakes away and steps back to the ball for a jumper at the top (both wings should rebound)

Coaching Points

- Players switch lines so that guards will rebound and posts will fill the lanes.
- Players should call out lanes when running and run as wide as possible.
- Using cones ensures that players run wide in the lanes.
- Coaches at the top of the key can force jump stops outside the lane.
- Players should run the fast break as quickly as possible without hurrying or being out of control.

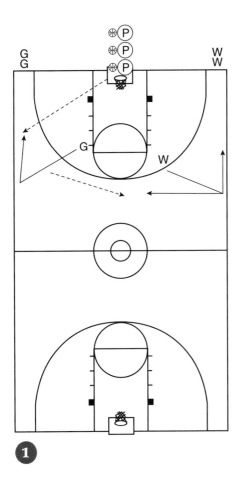

1

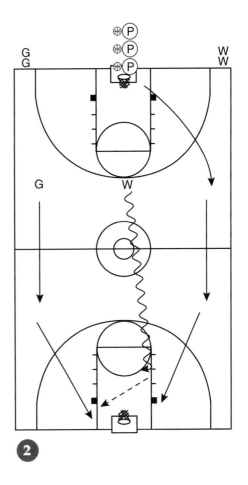

2

THREE-ON-TWO-ON-ONE BREAK

Joan Bonvicini | *University of Arizona*

Purpose

To teach a live fast break with an advantage to the offense. Players learn to read defenses, and the defense learns to force jump shots and prevent layups.

Organization

Two players line up at the half-court sideline on opposite sides. The rest of the team is in three lines on a baseline. The middle line has a ball.

Procedure

1. Run a three-player break off the backboard with an outlet pass. As the ball hits the backboard for a rebound, the two defenders come into the center circle and then backpedal playing tandem defense (see figure 1).
2. The three players on offense fill the three lanes and advance up the middle with the ball.
3. Once the ball crosses half-court, the offense should make no more than three passes before attempting a shot.
4. If a basket is made in the three-on-two situation, the shooter, for example O_1, becomes the defensive player, and the defense takes the ball out on the baseline.
5. Once a shot is attempted, all players should rebound. If the defense gets the rebound, the person who attempted the first shot sprints back to the other end for defense. The two defensive players become offensive players, and the drill is now a two-on-one situation going the other way. The two offensive players are now defensive players and wait for a new group at the half-court sideline (see figure 2).
6. Players proceed in a two-on-one and attempt to score.

Coaching Points

- Defenders in a three-on-two situation should be in a tandem defense. The top player stops the ball, and the bottom player defends the first pass.
- Players on offense in a three-on-two situation should move the ball quickly for a solid jumper or layup.
- Players on offense in a two-on-one situation should pass the ball quickly back and forth to force the defense to commit to them. They should always score on a layup.
- The defense in a two-on-one situation should fake at the offensive player and try to force her into a jump shot.

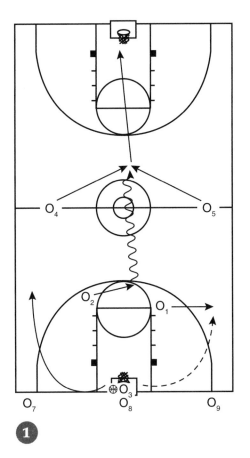

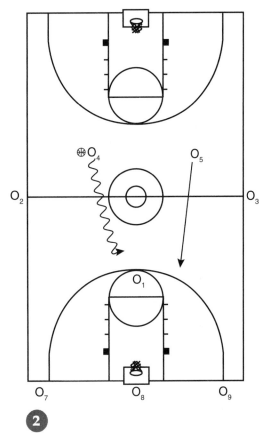

1

2

LEAD POST PASSING

Jon Newlee | *Idaho State University*

Purpose

To work on getting the ball up the court in transition with the long lead pass to the post for a layup.

Organization

Three defensive players start inside the key. A coach has a ball.

Procedure

1. The coach shoots and misses. The three players start in the key. The rebounder (O_1) makes an outlet pass to the guard (O_3), who runs to the free throw line extended. The post player who didn't get the rebound (O_2) sprints down the middle of the floor.

2. The guard (O_3) advances the ball up the sideline with one or two dribbles, then makes a long lead pass to the post player running down the middle of the floor for a layup (O_2). The rebounder (O_1) sprints down the floor after making the outlet pass to receive the ball out of the net after player O_2 makes the layup (if she misses, the rebounder gets the rebound and puts it in).

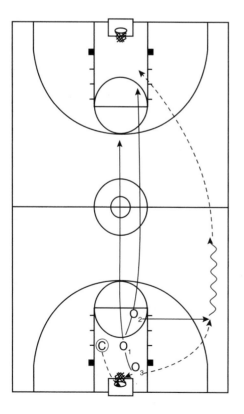

Coaching Points

- Emphasize grabbing the rebound at the highest point with two hands off the glass.
- Remind players to make crisp outlet passes, either a chest pass or over-the-head pass.
- Make sure that the post, who is the first one down, sprints to half-court, then looks over her shoulder for the pass from the guard.
- Make sure the pass to the post isn't too early. Players should not force the post players to put the ball on the floor. They should be able to catch the pass and go right up for a layup.

Variations

- Perform the drill with two guards and one post or two posts and one guard.
- Perform the drill in either direction. An outlet to the right should result in a right-handed layup, and an outlet pass to the left should result in a left-handed layup.
- Run the drill with the final outcome being a pass to the trailing post or guard for the three-point shot.

Jon Newlee | *Idaho State University*

Purpose
To simulate transition from defense to offense on a defensive rebound. To improve conditioning and agility. This is a great warm-up drill.

Organization
A coach with a ball stands at the free throw line, two players (O_1 and O_2) are on each side of the basket at the low block, one of them with a ball. The other players are lined up on the lane lines toward the free throw line.

Procedure
1. On the whistle, players O_1 and O_2 tip the ball off the glass to each other as they are in the air. This continues for about 15 seconds. The ball should not hit the floor or the rim.
2. When the coach blows the whistle again, either player O_1 or O_2 tips the ball off the glass one more time.
3. The next players in line step in immediately and continue the drill by tipping the ball off the glass to each other. A player in each group should have a basketball, and each group should be ready to start as soon as the group in front clears out.
4. Players O_1 and O_2 sprint down in transition, making sure they get wide. The coach with the ball makes an outlet pass to player O_1 or O_2, usually the first player out of the paint and to the wing area.

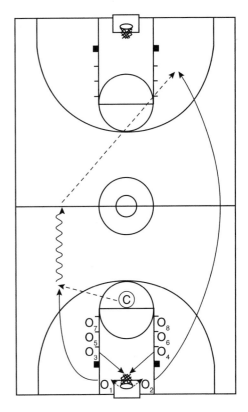

5. The player who received the outlet pass advances the ball up the court and delivers a crosscourt pass to the other player for a layup. Coaches can customize the finish of this drill to fit with the principles of their transition game.

Coaching Points
- Emphasize getting wide when filling the lanes.
- Demand that players make crisp, hard passes that lead their teammates up the floor.
- Remind players to finish the drill by going hard through the layup.

Variations
- Players penetrate the baseline for a corner three-point shot.
- Players execute a give-and-go.

Defensive Skills

chapter 10

Footwork Drills

If you believe the adage "offense sells tickets, but defense wins games," then you should also know that sound footwork is the basis for any successful defense. Footwork can be taught, learned, and improved more than any other skill, yet it is often overlooked for other parts of the game.

Successful players in today's game have sound footwork and depend on it heavily to get them into proper position for on-ball or off-ball coverage responsibilities. They may also have outstanding quickness, great leaping ability, or incredible anticipation, but the best defenders all have outstanding footwork.

The drills presented in this section and throughout the book are from the top defensive coaches in the country. Follow their breakdowns and learn how to make footwork fun, challenging, and rewarding. These coaches expect to develop excellent players with the defensive abilities that win games. Build your program similarly, and perhaps you'll enjoy the rewards and longevity that go with the knowledge that "offense sells tickets, but defense wins games."

Jane Albright I Wichita State University

Purpose
To teach proper footwork for defending the low post when fronting or going over the top.

Organization
Use four players and one ball.

Procedure
1. Start with the offensive and defensive players in low post on the left side and two passers on the perimeter at the wing and baseline.
2. Start the ball at the wing. The defender is in three-quarter denial on the high side of the low post.
3. On a pass to the baseline, the defender steps over the offense with her right foot to the front, then the post. She reverse pivots on her right foot and pulls her left foot through to deny on the baseline side.
4. On a pass from the baseline back to the wing, her left foot steps through to the front post, and then she pulls her right foot through and back to the original three-quarter denial position.

Coaching Points
- The defender should keep space between herself and the offensive player to prevent her from posting the defender up or pinning on a reverse pass.
- Players should move on the pass. Using two quick steps is the most efficient.

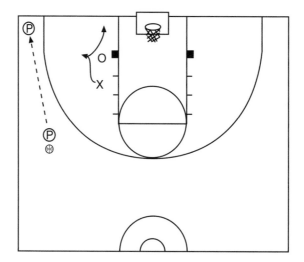

CHASE

Jane Albright ∣ *Wichita State University*

Purpose

To develop defensive quickness, balance, and the ability to change directions quickly.

Organization

Use four players and four cones.

Procedure

1. Start one player at each cone.
2. Players sprint from cone A to B.
3. Players slide from cone B to C.
4. Players backpedal from cone C to D.
5. Players slide from cone D to A.
6. Players try to catch the person in front of them; if they are successful, the player who was caught drops out. Play until one player is left or for a set time.

Coaching Points

- Players should stay low on slides, keeping the feet apart.
- Players should keep the weight forward on the backpedal to avoid falling back.
- Players stay outside of the cones.

Variation

Reverse directions: Sprint from cone D to C, slide from cone C to B, backpedal from cone B to A, and slide from cone A to D.

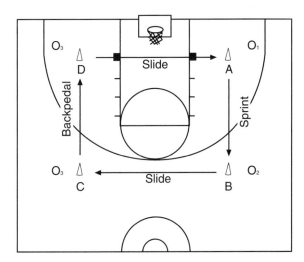

LANE CLOSEOUT

Jane Albright | Wichita State University

Purpose

To work on different aspects of defense, such as slides, closeouts, backpedals, and sprints. To close out under control, without lunging.

Organization

Two to three players under each basket start on the baseline.

Procedure

1. One player at a time starts on the baseline or on the right side facing the foul line. The player closes out against an imaginary offensive player on the right side, faces with her foot toward the imaginary player, and backpedals to the baseline, with her hands above her head.
2. She closes out to the foul line again. This time she pivots and sprints to the basket, then jumps up to touch the backboard or net.
3. She closes out a third time to the foul line. She touches it with her foot, drop-steps, and slides to the baseline.
4. The next player starts.
5. Repeat these three steps three times.

Coaching Points

- On the closeout, players should sprint out and shuffle to the foul line on the last step or two, with hands high.
- Players should stay balanced on the backpedal and low on the slides.
- Players should maintain the proper closeout position while moving, with the body always in control.

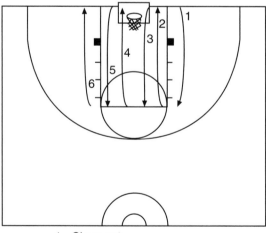

1 Close out
2 Backpedal
3 Close out
4 Sprint and touch backboard/net
5 Close out
6 Drop step–slide

CLOSEOUT

Cindy Griffin | Saint Joseph's University

Purpose

To improve defenders' helpside defense by recovering quickly. To close out the shooter and react to dribble penetration.

Organization

Half of the team lines up at each end under the basket. A coach with a ball is at each end.

Procedure

1. The first two players in line step out. The offensive player is at the wing outside the three-point line.
2. The defensive player is in help position and able to see both the ball and player.
3. The coach has the ball at the three-point line on the opposite wing.
4. The coach makes a skip pass to the offensive player, who tries to shoot or drive.
5. The defensive player closes out on offense (runs out) with a high hand close enough to prevent a shot.
6. The defensive player forces the ball to the corner.

Coaching Points

- Players should stay low on the closeout. They should not hop or jump-stop into the offense.
- Players should hold the high hand straight up and keep the butt down.
- Offensive players should drive to the baseline, but not open too much.

Variations

- Use posts in this drill to work on mobility and zone slides.
- Box out and rebound to work on playing hard to the end.

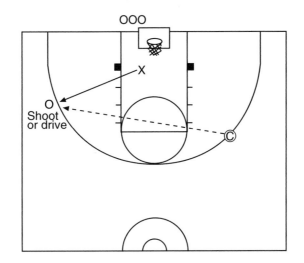

Cindy Griffin I Saint Joseph's University

Purpose
To help players recover when getting beat off the dribble.

Organization
Use four players (two on offense, two on defense), one ball, and a coach on the wing.

Procedure
1. The coach passes the ball to O_1 (X_1 denies this but lets the offense catch the ball for the sake of the drill).
2. Player O_1 beats X_1 off the dribble going to her left.
3. Player X_2 drop-steps off her player and slides over to stop the ball penetration of O_1.
4. Once the ball is stopped, X_1 can recover to her player, and X_2 goes back to denying player O_2 the ball.
5. Repeat from several angles to the basket (e.g., wing to post, post to post, guard to post).

Coaching Points
- Players should stay low, keep their hands active, communicate on screens, and maintain balance.
- The defender who loses the ball should communicate that she has recovered so that her teammate can go back to her player.
- Players should communicate.

Variation
Advance to three-on-three; help and recover using the same principles.

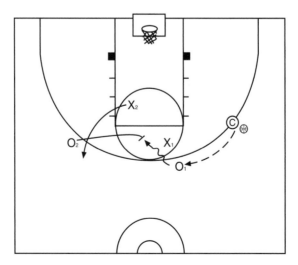

PERIMETER CLOSEOUT

Kris Huffman | *DePauw University*

Purpose

To help defensive players improve closeout technique and positioning. The defender attempts to take away the outside shot, the look inside, and the middle penetration with the pressure she applies.

Organization

Use 12 players and five balls. A coach at the top of the key passes the ball. Three offensive players line up on each side of the three-point line; three defenders start in the lane. The next three defenders are ready to enter the lane when it is vacated.

Procedure

1. The coach slaps the ball to start the drill. The three defenders in the lane drop into a stance and stutter step.
2. The coach passes to one side or the other. The three defenders close out to the offensive players.
3. The top offensive player passes back to the coach. The three defenders jump to the ball, then become the offensive players. The offensive players join the defensive line on the baseline.
4. The next three defenders are in the lane stuttering. The coach passes to the other side and the drill continues.

Coaching Points

- The defenders must close out in a stance with the inside foot and hand up.
- The offensive players must be active with the ball and provide a triple threat. They must jab while the defender pressures the ball.

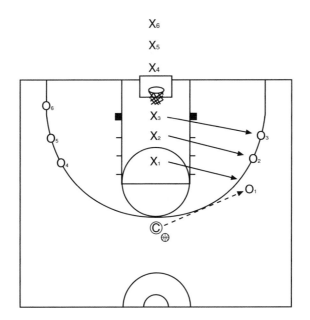

SUPER DENIAL

Muffet McGraw | *University of Notre Dame*

Purpose
To improve the players' reaction time from denying a pass to the wing to defending the backdoor cut.

Organization
Use one offensive player on the wing, one offensive player on the block, one defensive player denying on the wing, and one coach with a rack of balls at the top of the key.

Procedure
1. The coach makes a pass to the wing. The defender knocks the pass away and immediately slides or shuffles to the block to defend the pass from the coach to the block (see figure 1).
2. After knocking the pass away to the block, the defender slides or shuffles back to knock away the pass to the wing (see figure 2).
3. Repeat for a total of five deflections.

Coaching Points
- Emphasize quickly turning the head, pushing off hard with the outside leg, and keeping the hand out in the passing lane.
- Use a rack of balls so you can fire the passes quickly.
- Make the defender work to get the deflection, but do not let her cross her feet or run.

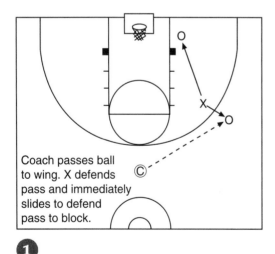

Coach passes ball to wing. X defends pass and immediately slides to defend pass to block.

1

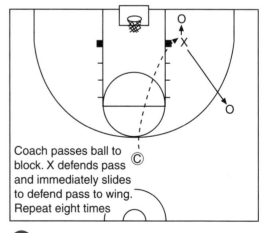

Coach passes ball to block. X defends pass and immediately slides to defend pass to wing. Repeat eight times

2

TURN AND CHANNEL

Pat Summitt | *University of Tennessee*

Purpose

To teach players how to pick up the ball full court, force the dribbler to turn at least once before the ball gets to half-court, then channel the offensive player down the sideline.

Organization

Use as many pairs of players as you like. Each pair of players has a ball.

Procedure

1. Pair up players with similar physical abilities.
2. The offensive player begins to dribble up the floor.
3. The defensive player gets in the offensive player's way and makes her change direction.
4. The defensive player tries to force two or three turns.
5. Once the ball is across the half-court line, the defender channels the offensive player down the sideline.
6. The offensive player tries to beat the defenders down the middle.

Coaching Points

- The dribbler should start slow and make turns whether she is forced or not.
- The defender should get in front of the dribbler with her head on the ball.
- The defender should not allow the dribbler to go across the floor in the half-court.

Variation

Once the players know how the drill works, have the offensive player go full speed to see if the defender can influence where the ball goes.

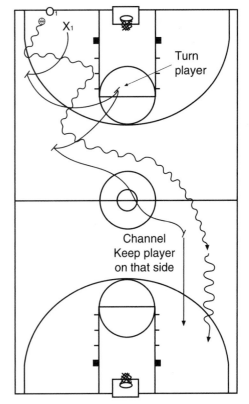

ONE-ON-ONE FULL COURT

Tim Shea | *Salem State College*

Purpose

To teach players how to prevent dribblers from getting by them.

Organization

Two players (one offensive and one defensive) and one ball are on each side of the court. The rest of the players are on the baseline, and a coach is in the middle of the court.

Procedure

1. The offensive player tries to get by her defender. If she does, she speed dribbles to the end of the court.
2. The defender forces the dribbler to use her weak hand at all times.
3. Each pair of players must stay between the sideline and the free throw lane extended on their side of the court. The coaches stand in the middle of the court.
4. Players switch offense to defense at the far end of the court for the return trip.
5. Each player goes three times. Coaches should run this drill every other practice.

Coaching Points

- These defensive principles are for use on the perimeter only, not in scoring areas.
- A defender is most likely to be beaten on a dribbler's initial move. The defender should back off until the dribbler puts the ball on the floor, then tighten up the distance between the defender and the ball.
- Once a defender learns how far off the ball she should be, she must maintain that distance. If the dribbler gets too close, the defender does not have the correct spacing.
- When a dribbler gets going with her weak hand, the defender should not shut her down, which will allow her to use her strong hand. Instead, the defender should stay in a defensive position and allow the dribbler to keep going, using her weak hand.
- Players should go against different opponents each time.
- This drill is an excellent dribbling drill, too.

Variation

Try to force the dribbler to change direction as many times as possible, but do not let the dribbler beat the defense.

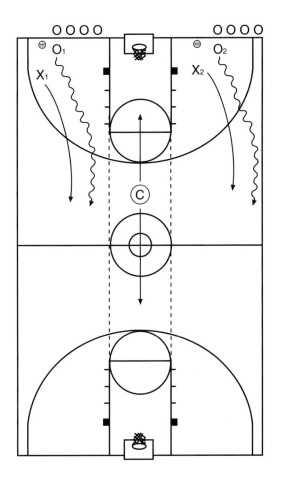

John Margaritis | University of California at Riverside

Purpose

To teach a combination of defensive responsibilities.

Organization

Use two offensive players, one defensive player, two passers, a coach, and one ball. The passers could be managers or other players.

Procedure

1. Start the drill with the coach handling the ball, trying to pass to O_1. X_1 tries to deny the entry pass to O_1 (see figure 1).
2. If the coach completes the pass to O_1, O_1 may drive the ball to the basket. She is allowed up to three dribbles, but she may not shoot. Player O_1 may also return the ball to the coach or to one of the passers.
3. When the coach has the ball, X_1 follows ballside responsibilities as she denies the coach's pass to O_1.
4. When P_1 has the ball, X_1 jumps to midline and establishes helpside responsibility by creating a flat triangle (see figure 2).
5. When P_2 has the ball, X_1 slides across the lane and denies the ballside, low-post O_2 (see figure 3). In a game situation, X_1 may double-team O_2. We exaggerate by asking X_1 to deny O_2.
6. When O_2 or P_2 passes the ball back on top to P_1, X_1 reestablishes her flat triangle with O_1, and X_1 is now allowed to flash-cut through the lane (see figure 4). X_1 should bump the flash cut as if trying to draw a charge and force O_1 to go above her or below her. If O_1 goes above her toward the top of the key, O_1 stays in a closed stance and denies to the thee-point line. If O_1 cuts backdoor, X_1 snaps her head and denies the low-post cut from the high side.
7. Meanwhile, if P_1 passes to the coach, X_1 resumes ballside defense and denies the entry pass to O_1.

Coaching Point

- During the drill, the coach constantly instructs X_1 on proper denial and help side techniques.
- X_1 goes through the drill for a period of time, and then players rotate until everyone has played defense.

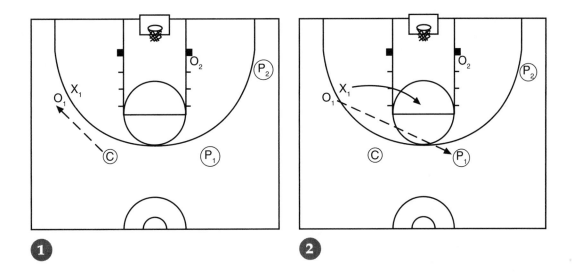

1

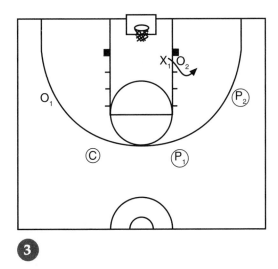

3

4

chapter 11

Defensive Screening Drills

Screen-and-roll, give-and-go, dive-and-cut—without these tactics how would an offense begin to attack a strong defensive team? Most scouting reports can give a coach the patterns and tendencies of an opponent, but nothing can replace the day-to-day drilling that players must complete and the preparation that players must have to be able to read and react properly to screening situations.

Top programs owe much of their defensive success to reading and reacting properly in game screening situations. Motion offenses give players a lot of freedom that can challenge an unprepared defensive team. However, communication, anticipation, team concept, and unselfish play allow players to apply pressure or provide help at just the right time.

In this chapter, you'll learn how to break down an opponent's screen and take them out of their offensive patterns. Daily drilling on your screening principles will allow players to feel comfortable in any situation, knowing they can depend on one another to communicate, anticipate, and play unselfishly.

UCLA CUTTING

Cindy Griffin | *Saint Joseph's University*

Purpose

To defend front cuts and work on jumping to the ball.

Organization

Divide the team into two groups. One group is lined up at the top of each key with a ball.

Procedure

1. Player O_1 has the ball, and player X_1 is defending, forcing O_1 to the corner.
2. Player O_1 passes to the coach on the wing and tries to front-cut.
3. Player X_1 jumps to the ball and forces O_1 to cut behind her.
4. Player X_1 opens up to the ball, following O_1 down the lane.
5. The coach tries to pass to O_1.
6. Player X_1 needs a deflection or a steal to get off the court.

Coaching Points

- The defense needs to stay low.
- The defense needs to follow and feel the offense through, seeing the ball at the same time.

Variations

- Player O_1 posts up on the block; player X_1 needs to front.
- The offensive cutting line is at the wing (where the coach was), and the coach is in the corner. The pass goes to the coach. The offense tries to front out; the defender jumps to the ball and forces the offense to cut behind.

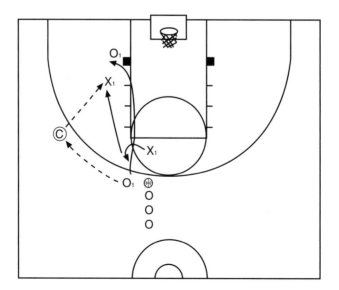

STEP BACK, GET THROUGH

Cindy Griffin | Saint Joseph's University

Purpose
To get through screens occurring off the ball.

Organization
Three offensive players and three defenders are at one end of the court. The three offensive players start with the ball at the top, and two defenders are in the wings.

Procedure
1. Player O_2 passes to O_1 and screens for O_3.
2. Player X_2 steps back and lets X_3 (who is getting screened) through.
3. Once X_3 gets through, she must be on the line or up the line to prevent the curl cut to the basket by O_3.
4. Player X_1 maintains good guarding position on the O_1 passer.

Coaching Points
- Players must communicate on impending screens.
- Players should help teammates through the screen by stepping back and pulling their shirts to help them get by.
- Players should recover in the passing lane, ready to prevent the cutter from receiving the ball.

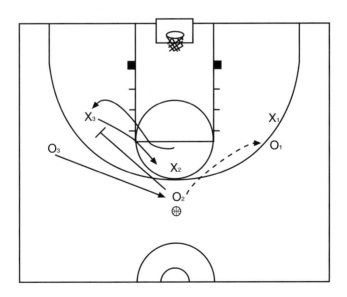

Nikki Caldwell | *University of Tennessee*

Purpose

To help players recognize and defend screens on the ball with rotation from the help side.

Organization

Use six players, three offensive and three defensive on the perimeter, and one ball.

Procedure

1. Players are three on three on the perimeter.
2. Player O_1 passes to either O_2 or O_3. Player O_1 then goes to set a screen on the ball (see figure 1).
3. Weakside defense jumps to the help side.
4. The player on the wing with the ball uses the screen and attacks the middle.
5. The defensive player on the ball and the defensive player guarding the person setting the screen trap the wing (see figure 2).
6. The weakside defender on the help side reads the situation and tries to steal the pass made to the person who has rolled off the screen.
7. Players don't give up a layup. The weakside defender must play both her player and the person who has set the screen.
8. If the pass is made out of the trap, the defensive player who was initially screened rotates out of the trap and finds the open player.

Coaching Points

- The weakside defender gets off to the help side. She tries to steal the ball, but doesn't give up a layup.
- Defense must communicate on all screens.
- Players should set a good trap without allowing the offense to split the trap.

Variation

Three-on-three could consist of a player up top, a player on the wing, and a player on the block.

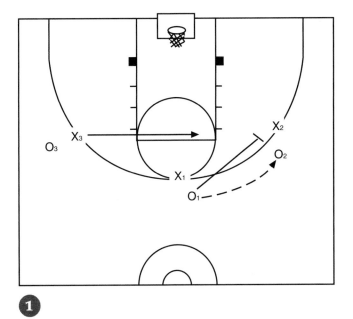

1

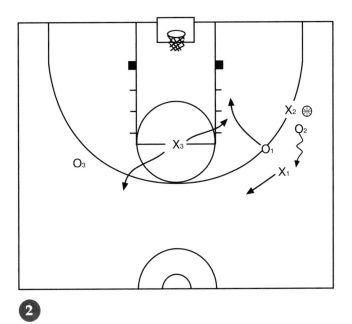

2

BREAK THE BACK SCREEN

Andy Landers | *University of Georgia*

Purpose

To teach players to set, use, and defend back screens.

Organization

Use two offensive and two defensive players, one on the wing and one on the block, and one coach with the ball.

Procedure

1. Player O_1 drives her player away from the impending screen from O_2, setting up her player.
2. Player O_2 comes up to screen for O_1 (giving one step to her defender if this is a blind-screen rule).
3. Player O_2 screens X_1 from the rear. Player O_1 makes a quick, hard cut to the basket.
4. Player O_2 rolls back toward the ball after screening.
5. Player X_1 and X_2 communicate and work together to defend the screen.

Coaching Points

- Players should give the defender a step to avoid contact on all blind or rear screens.
- Players should roll back to the ball after screening defense.

Variation

Players can combine double screens and back screens into one drill, teaching communication and taking it into two-on-two play.

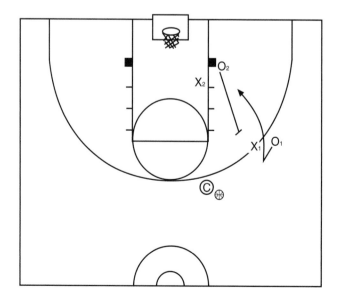

DEFENDING DOWN SCREENS

Andy Landers | *University of Georgia*

Purpose

To teach players how to set down screens and how to defend these screens.

Organization

Use two lines (one out of bounds near the block and the other on the wing) and one coach with the ball at the top. Play two on two, with offense and defense on the wing and underneath.

Procedure

1. Player O_1 starts on the wing and comes down to set the screen for O_2 on the block.
2. Player O_2 gets her defender (X_2) up by driving her under the basket, then waiting for the screen to be set before cutting hard off the screen.
3. Player O_1 rolls back toward the coach with the ball.
4. The defenders communicate and work together to get through screens.
5. The offense goes to defense, and the defensive players go to the ends of different offensive lines.

Coaching Points

- Players should set up the defensive player by driving her under the basket as the screen is being set.
- The screener should put her belly button on the hip of the defender.
- The screener always rolls back to the ball.

Variation

Play two on two live after a certain number of down screens.

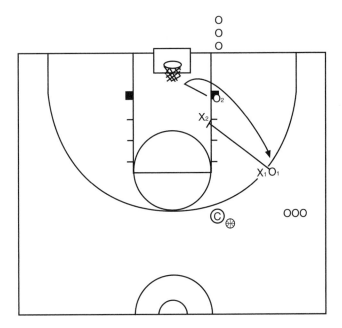

Andy Landers | *University of Georgia*

Purpose

To teach players how to set legal screens for a ball handler, how to roll to get open, and how to defend the screens.

Organization

Use three offensive players, three defensive players, one ball, and lines of players behind each of the three offensive players. Start one offensive player at the top of the key and one on each wing.

Procedure

1. Player O_1 starts with the ball at the top and passes to O_2 (see figure 1).
2. Player O_1 follows the pass and screens on the ball for O_2.
3. Player O_2 dribbles over the screen. Player O_1 rolls hard (defense may fight over the top or step through—the coach's philosophy dictates).
4. Player O_2 gets to the top and passes to O_3 (see figure 2).
5. Player O_2 follows the pass and screens on the ball for O_3. Player O_2 rolls.
6. Continue for four or five repetitions and rotate offense to defense and defense to the back of a different line.

Coaching Points

- Remind players to set a solid, strong screen with the belly button on the hip.
- Remind the defense to communicate in order to deal with screens effectively.
- Work with defense on getting over screens, switching, or sliding under.
- Emphasize the roll, good contact, and the target hand.

Variations

- Have players hit the roll with a pass if open; defense defends.
- Play three on three live after four screens.

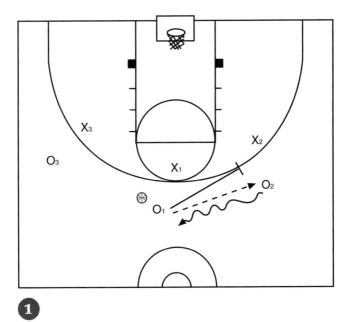

1

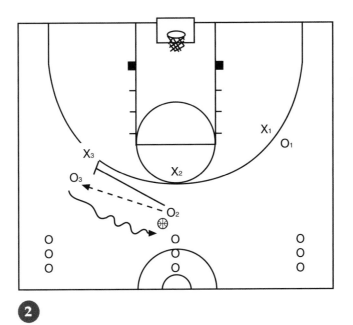

2

Kay Yow | *North Carolina State University*

Purpose

To learn to defend a back screen using player-to-player principles and to recognize guard–guard, post–post, or guard–post screens.

Organization

Use two offensive players, two defensive players, one ball, and a line of players under the basket. Players are positioned on both the left elbow and left block, and a coach is positioned at the top of the key with a ball. Another coach is on the right wing. Players rotate up the line (defense on block to offense on block, offense on block to defense on elbow, defense on elbow to offense on elbow, offense on elbow to the end of the line).

Procedure

1. Players X_1 and X_2 take proper defensive positions in relation to the ball at the top of the key (see figure 1).
2. The coach passes the ball to the coach on the right wing. Players X_1 and X_2 adjust their positions in relation to the ball and their defensive assignments.
3. As the coach on the wing receives the ball, O_2 sets a back screen for O_1 on the elbow (see figure 2).
4. Player X_2 gets as close to O_2 as possible, leaving X_1 plenty of room to get through the screen. (As an option, depending on the offensive player, X_2 may drop off O_2 and put a hand in the passing lane until X_1 recovers to O_1. Player X_2 then recovers to O_2.)
5. Player X_1 rolls off the screen toward the ball with her hand up in the passing lane and meets O_1 on the block (see figures 3 and 4).
6. Player X_2 helps X_1 if O_1 flares or kicks back off the screen.
7. If O_1 flares or kicks back, X_2 and X_1 help and recover quickly.

Note: If the screen is guard–guard or post–post, simply switch on the screen.

Coaching Points

- Players must communicate, letting teammates know the screen is coming, and recognize the type of screen (guard–guard, post–post, or guard–post).
- Using proper player-to-player defensive positions, players should try to avoid the screen altogether.
- If help is required, players should help and recover quickly.
- The defender being screened must always roll toward the ball with her hand up. This player needs to look big and cut down the passing angle.
- The player guarding the screener can help slow the offensive player using the screen by bumping the cutter.

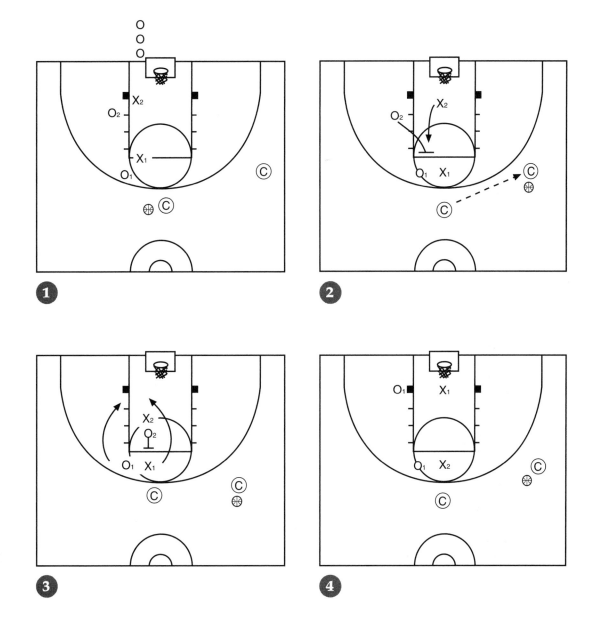

1

2

3

4

CONTINUOUS CROSS SCREENS

Kay Yow | *North Carolina State University*

Purpose

To teach players to stay with their defensive assignments on screens that occur away from the ball by using solid player-to-player principles and positioning.

Organization

Use three lines, one at the top of the key and one on each wing. The first player in each line is defense, and the next player is offense. The offensive player at the top of the key starts the drill with a ball. Offense goes to defense, and defense rotates clockwise to the end of the next line.

Procedure

1. Player O_1 passes to O_2 (see figure 1).
2. All the defensive players adjust their positions based on where the ball is.
3. After passing, O_1 goes away from the ball to set a screen on X_3.
4. Player X_1 sags toward the basket in her help spot as O_1 goes away from the ball. Player X_1 needs to be sure to leave X_3 enough room to slide through the screen.
5. Player X_3 takes a step backward toward the basket and slides through the screen to beat, or at least meet, O_3 at the top of the key (see figure 2).
6. Player X_3 is in a position to steal or knock the ball away (see figure 3).

Coaching Points

- Teach proper body position and angles.
- Stress the fundamentals of proper player-to-player defense. The defensive players must reposition themselves on every pass and jump to the ball.
- Teach players to see the screen coming so they can avoid the screen altogether.
- Stress the importance of communication between teammates.

Variation

Have the wings V-cut to get open and receive the ball. Once the screen is set, play live (three on three). Offense can score only off a cross screen.

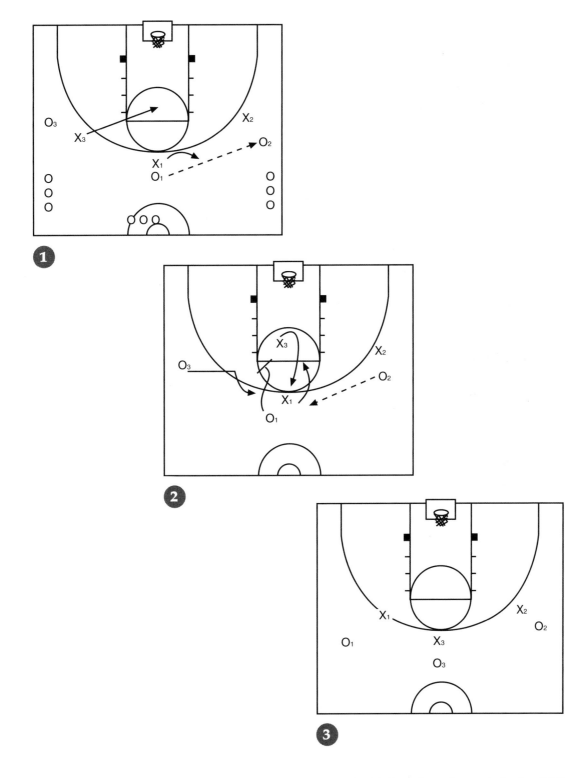

Charlene Thomas-Swinson | *University of Tulsa*

Purpose

To teach players to stay with their assignment and be aware of how to defend away from the ball.

Organization

Use three offensive players and three defensive players. A coach is at a wing for passing.

Procedure

1. Player O_1 starts with the ball and passes to the coach. All defenders jump to the ball in a denial with a one- or two-pass defensive stance (see figure 1).
2. Players O_1 and O_2 set a stagger screen for O_3. Players X_1 and X_2 alert X_3 that a screen is coming.
3. Player X_3 adjusts her stance, chases O_3 to the top of the key, and positions herself to delay and deflect the pass to O_3 (see figure 2).
4. The coach passes the ball to O_3, and they play until there is a defensive stop (see figure 3).

Coaching Points

- Players should use proper positioning, angles off of the ball, and on-ball defense.
- Stress the importance of communication between teammates.
- Challenge players to work together to get a defensive stop.

Variation

Challenge offensive players to use a change of speed to get open off of the stagger screen. Offense can only score off of the screen, so if they aren't open, give them two tries with the drill and then rotate new players in.

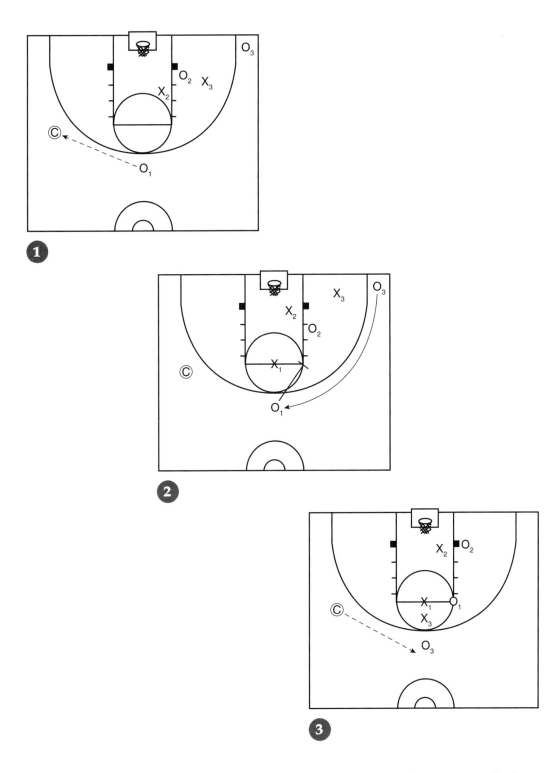

Charlene Thomas-Swinson | *University of Tulsa*

Purpose

To teach players how to defend against two screens that are happening simultaneously while still being able to delay and disrupt their opponent from scoring.

Organization

Use two players to set the screen and two players to defend. Use a coach as the passer.

Procedure

1. Player O_1 passes the ball to the coach. X_1 jumps into a high-side denial stance (see figure 1).
2. The coach dribbles over, and X_1 opens up in order to see her player and the ball (see figure 2).
3. Player O_1 runs to use the double screen she is receiving from O_2 and O_3.
4. Player X_1 chases O_1 as tightly as she can. Player X_1 defends O_1 and steps into a denial stance in order to delay or deflect the pass (see figure 3).
5. If O_1 gets the ball, X_1 contests and boxes out O_1's shot.
6. Offense becomes defense, and the drill starts over (see figure 4).

Coaching Point

Make sure that all players have the opportunity to run this drill so that they have an understanding of the angles needed. Since dribbling is not allowed, the offense will be forced to come off of the screen ready to catch and score.

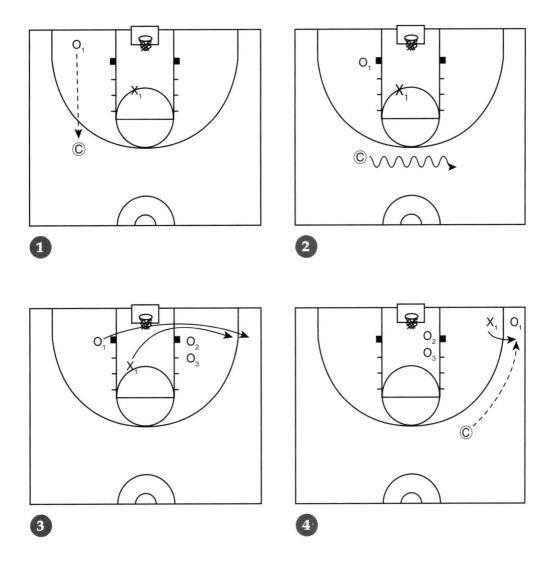

Charlene Thomas-Swinson | *University of Tulsa*

Purpose

To teach players to defend their man away from the ball when a flare screen is received, and how to position themselves to defend it.

Organization

Use four players and a passer.

Procedure

1. Player O_1 passes the ball to the coach at the wing (see figure 1). Player X_1 jumps to a denial stance one pass away. Player X_2 jumps into a two-pass-away help stance.
2. Player O_2 sets a flare screen for O_1. Player X_2 lets X_1 know about the screen, and opens up to allow X_1 to step under the screen or go over the top of the screen (see figure 2).
3. Player X_2 recovers and gets into a denial stance to defend O_2.
4. The drill is done twice, and then the players rotate.

Coaching points

- Work to get a defensive stop through the concept of staying between the ball and the basket to delay or disrupt the offense.
- Only allow the offense two dribbles to score.

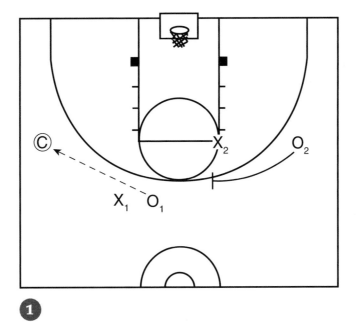

1

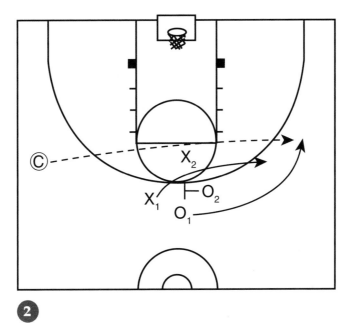

2

DEFENDING BALL SCREENS

Kay Yow | North Carolina State University

Purpose

To force the ball handler out wide and allow the defender time to fight over the top of the screen.

Organization

Use two defensive players, two offensive players, one ball, and the rest of the players in two lines. Guards are in a line at the wing, and posts are in a line under the basket near the block. The first person in line is defense and the second person in line is offense. Players rotate from offense to defense to the end of their line.

Procedure

1. Players X_1 and X_2 take proper player-to-player positions, based on the position of the ball and their defensive assignments.
2. Player O_2 sets a screen on the ball for O_1. Player O_1 tries to use the screen and get to the basket.
3. Player X_2 gets to the high side of the screen, forcing the ball handler to take an arched path to the basket.
4. Player X_1 turns and sprints through the screen and beats the ball handler to the spot, preventing her from turning the corner and getting to the basket.
5. Player X_2 has helped and must recover quickly as X_1 recovers back to the ball.

Note: If the screen is guard–guard or post–post, switch on the screen.

Coaching Points

- Good timing as well as good communication between players is essential.
- Post player hedging must be at a 90-degree angle to the direction the ball handler is heading. If the body position is too open, the dribbler will have a direct path to the basket.
- The defender on the ball must turn and sprint through the screen to the spot that the ball handler is heading to. Sliding is too slow.
- The post player must never lose touch with her defensive assignment. She should keep one hand on the offensive player's hip and the other out, up, and wide.

Variations

- Perform the drill from various spots on the floor.
- Have the guard on the ball go behind the screen as the post player bodies up.
- Have players trap the ball handler.

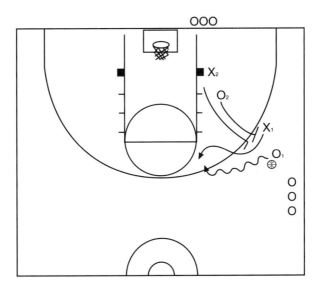

STEPPING IN ON THE BALL

John Margaritis | *University of California at Riverside*

Purpose

To teach players how to defend the on-ball screen.

Organization

Use six players: three on offense and three on defense.

Procedure

1. Players O_1 and X_1 are at the top of the key. Players O_2 and X_2 are on one wing, and players O_3 and X_3 are on the other (see figure 1).
2. Player O_1 dribbles the ball toward the wing. Player O_3 comes toward the ball and sets an on-ball screen. Player X_3 recognizes and calls out the screen as she adjusts her position from playing between player O_3 and the basket to stepping above player O_3 and in the path of the dribbler, player O_1 (see figure 2).
3. Player X_3 must accomplish one of four objectives:
   - Make the dribbler go wider to give player X_1 room to slide through and stay with player O_1.
   - Make player O_1 dribble back to where she came from.
   - Force player O_1 to pick up the ball.
   - Draw a charge.
4. To continue the drill, player O_1 dribbles toward the other wing and receives an on-ball screen from player O_2. Player X_2 steps in on the ball and defends the on-ball screen (see figure 3).
5. After player O_1 has dribbled back and forth a few times, players rotate counterclockwise and finally offense to defense.

Coaching Points

- When player X_3 tries to make the dribbler go wide, she should place her body at the same angle and next to player O_3, as if there were two people setting a screen. When player O_1 is forced to go higher than the screen to avoid contact with player X_3, player X_3 reverse pivots on the foot closest to the screener to create the space that player X_1 needs to slide through.
- When player X_3 tries to make player O_1 dribble back to where she came from, player X_1 should not be overly anxious to get over the screen. Her responsibility is to avoid getting beat on the side away from the screen.

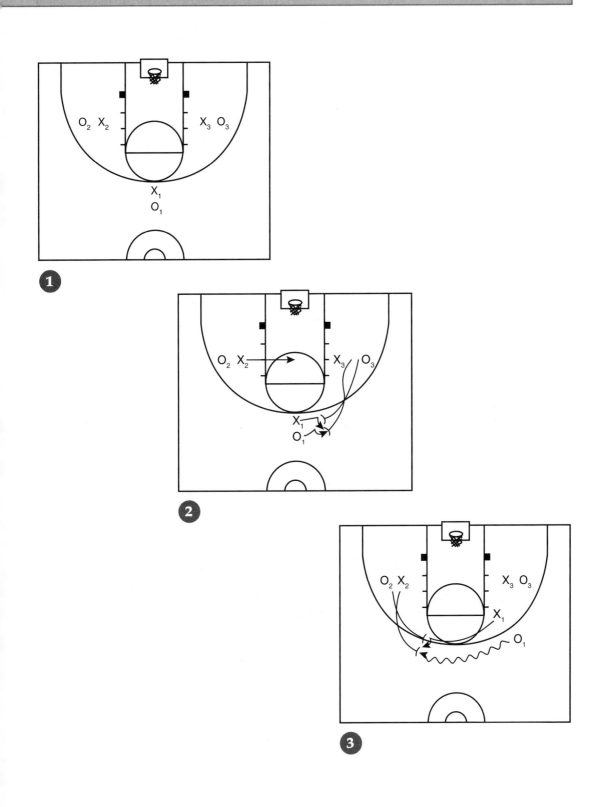

chapter 12

Defensive Rebounding Drills

Although it's obvious that big, strong, and tall players form a good rebounding team, we've also seen our share of small, aggressive, and hard-nosed teams dominate the boards, allowing their opponents no second shots. Defensive rebounding is both attitude and technique. A team of individuals, each dedicated to her rebounding assignment and with the commitment and ability to make sure her player does not get the ball, can frustrate a bigger, even taller, team no end.

Teaching the basic footwork of rebounding and the inevitability of contact goes a long way toward building your team's defensive framework. Being physically big or small has nothing to do with the size of your team's heart and their commitment to making sure their player does not get to a rebounded ball first.

Use the drills and techniques in this chapter to refine your defensive rebounding. These coaches know how to get the most out of their players and how to keep them focused on controlling the boards. Perhaps you'll pick up an idea that can help your players—big or small—earn the rebounds they deserve.

Carey Green | *Liberty University*

Purpose

To teach a defender on the block to go from playing three-quarter deny defense to good rebounding position.

Organization

A coach is at the top of the key with a ball. Two offensive players are on each block with a defender guarding each. The defensive players are playing three-quarter high side, using the hand farthest from the offense to deny the pass to the post.

Procedure

1. The coach tries to pass the ball to either offensive player in the post. The defenders try not to allow this pass. If nothing is open, the coach shoots the ball from the free throw line.
2. The defenders use their inside hand to push the offense away from the basket, and at the same time they turn and put their butts into the offensive player, pushing them back with the lower body.
3. Both the offense and defense go for the rebound.

Coaching Points

- Initially focus on good defensive position. The tendency is for players to worry about the rebound and play insufficient defense
- Emphasize rebounding position: staying low, pushing the offense back, making a quick low spin into the offense, and keeping the hands up in the air on the box-out to be ready for the rebound
- Have offensive players work on quick movements to get around the defender and get the rebound.

Variations

- Move the offense and defense up to the elbows. The defense still denies the pass to the offense, and the coach shoots from the three-point line.
- Position the offense and defense on the blocks, with the coach shooting from the wing. The defender on the block closest to the coach plays high-side deny, while the other defender is in help side. When the shot goes up, both defenders attempt to get in good rebounding position between their defender and the basket. This is more difficult for the strongside defender.

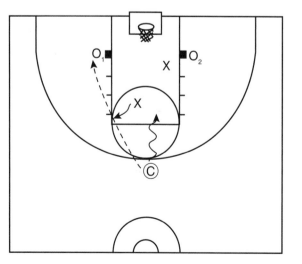

SKY AND FLY

Gary Blair | *Texas A&M University*

Purpose

To teach good rebounding habits and sound technique. To reinforce proper timing and execution of a rebound.

Organization

Two groups of rebounders line up on each side of the board; the first person in each line has a ball. The rest of the players form an outlet line on each side of the court.

Procedure

1. The first rebounder on each side tosses the ball off the glass and times the jump to catch the ball with both hands at the top of the jump.
2. After catching the ball, the rebounder pivots and passes to the player at the outlet on her side of the floor.
3. The rebounder follows her pass to the outlet. The outlet player goes to the back of the opposite rebounding line.
4. The next person in the rebounding line continues the drill.
5. Repeat until everyone has grabbed 10 boards.

Coaching Points

- Demand proper technique every time, otherwise it is wasted time.
- Remind players to Z the ball after grabbing the rebound with both hands to a chinned position. This keeps the ball moving and discourages others from reaching in.

Variations

- Start with the rebounder facing away from the backboard and have the next player in line toss the ball off the glass to force the rebounder to turn and find the ball.
- Allow the outlet passer to take the dribble to the other end for a shot. This maximizes the drill by adding conditioning and shooting.

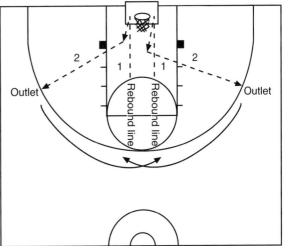

Gary Blair | *Texas A&M University*

Purpose

To simulate a game situation of half-court rebounding while encouraging the offense to crash the boards. It also improves conditioning.

Organization

Use a coach with the ball, three lines of players under the goal, and three offensive players and three defensive players on the court. A rebound ring creates realistic misses. You can use cones to mark where the players should sprint.

Procedure

1. Offense assumes their position on the court relative to where the coach is with the ball (see figure 1).
2. Defense matches up with offense and assumes the defensive position that the coach desires.
3. When the coach is satisfied with the defense's positioning, she or he takes the shot (see figure 2).
4. Defense calls "shot," and then they find, feel, and fly (find their player, feel the contact, and fly to the ball). Offense crashes the boards.
5. If defense controls, they outlet and go three on zero to other end. Then they sprint around the court to the back of the lines.
6. If offense controls, they power it back in. Defense must sprint to the other end, then around the court to the back of the lines.

Coaching Points

- Demand that defense be in the desired positions before offense takes the shot.
- Teach players to read and react to the shot. Long shots equal long rebounds. Sixty percent of the time, misses go to the weak side. Players should play the percentages.

Variations

- Move the shooter to various spots to change the rebound angles.
- Make the drill competitive by keeping score.

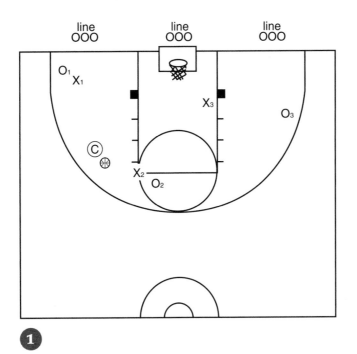

1

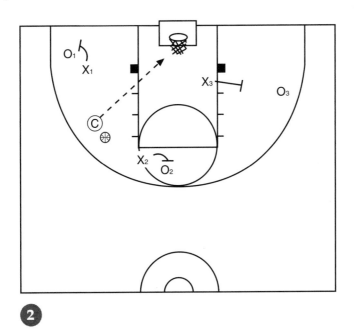

2

WEAKSIDE CRASHING

Gary Blair | *Texas A&M University*

Purpose

To teach players to crash weakside boards from game-situation positions. To teach players to read and react to shots so they can create more rebounding opportunities.

Organization

Use a rebound ring to create realistic misses. Use two offensive and two defensive players. A coach shoots from the wing. The rest of the players form two lines on the sidelines.

Procedure

1. The coach sets up 15 to 18 feet (4.5 to 5.5 meters) away on the wing area with the ball.
2. Two offensive players set up four to five steps outside the lane, opposite the coach.
3. Two defensive players assume good helpside defensive positions.
4. When the coach is satisfied with the position, she or he takes the shot.
5. The defense must find their players and keep them from getting pushed out of position.
6. If defense gets the rebound, they rotate to offense. Offense goes to the back of the line. If offense gets the rebound, they score. Defense must sprint to the other end, then to the back of the line.

Coaching Points

- Teach players to work from the off-ball defensive positions they would be in during a game.

- Teach defensive players to find their block-out responsibility, initiate the contact, and then go to the ball.

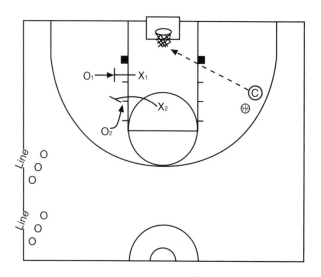

Variations

- Change the shot distances and angles to vary the rebounds.
- Substitute sprints with push-ups, jumps, or bleacher sprints.
- Make the drill competitive by keeping score.

130 WINNERS AND LOSERS

Kris Huffman | *DePauw University*

Purpose

To practice offensive and defensive rebounding technique. This drill also works on closing out and finishing under pressure.

Organization

Use 12 players in four lines at the corners of the lane (offensive players at elbows and defensive players on the baseline), one coach, and one ball.

Procedure

1. The coach passes to either offensive line. Both defenders close out.
2. The player with the ball must shoot upon receiving the ball.
3. The defenders box out. The drill becomes live two on two at this point.
4. Both offensive and defensive players try to rebound the shot, made or missed, and score.
5. The pair that scores wins (the first shot from the elbow doesn't count).
6. The winning pair gets in the defensive line on the baseline; the nonwinning pair lines up at the top of the key. After five minutes, the players who are lined up at the top of the key must run.

Coaching Points

- Both defenders must close out with the inside hand and foot up.
- Defenders must establish contact and gain good rebounding position.
- The shooter must go up strong and finish inside.

Variations

- When the drill becomes live two on two, limit the number of dribbles allowed.
- Vary the starting position of the offensive lines—midpost, wings, three-point shot, and so on.
- Allow the offensive player to drive after receiving the pass from the coach. This forces a good closeout.

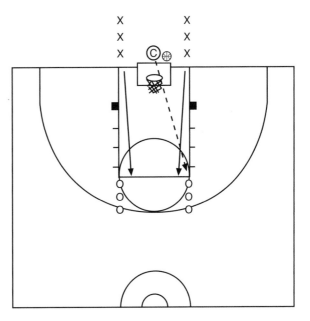

TRIANGLE BOX-OUT

Wendy Larry | *Old Dominion University*

Purpose
To practice rotation on box-outs when there is a front in the post.

Organization
Use three players on offense and three on defense, one coach, and one ball. One offensive player is at the ballside post, one is at the top of the key, and one is at the off-ball wing. Defense matches up, fronting the post.

Procedure
1. The coach bounces the ball to signal a rotation. Players rotate on each bounce. To start the drill the coach bounces once.
2. The off-ball defender rotates to the post defender's spot. The post defender moves to the top of the key, and the defender at the top of the key moves to off-ball defense. Offense does not move.
3. The coach bounces the ball up to three times and then shoots.
4. When there is a shot, there is a rotation; however, instead of getting in defensive positions, defenders box out the offensive player they rotate to. Offense crashes the boards hard.

Coaching Points
- The defense must get three rebounds in a row before changing to offense.
- The defense must get into good help defense position.
- Teamwork is key. If one person forgets to rotate, someone will be wide open for a rebound and put-back.

Variations
- Add another offensive and defensive player.
- Change the number of rebounds necessary for defense to change to offense.

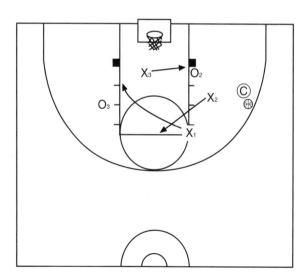

FOUR-PLAYER SHELL PROTECTION

Amy Ruley | *North Dakota State University*

Purpose

To teach defensive team rebounding, focusing on closing out, contesting shots, and blocking out.

Organization

Use one coach with the ball under the basket, four offensive players spread out in different shooting areas, and four defensive players facing their players in a defensive stance.

Procedure

1. The coach bounces the ball on the floor and passes to an offensive player. The defensive team slaps the floor, shouts "defense," then sprints to a closeout stance to contest the shooter or nonshooter.
2. The offensive rebounds are live. The defensive team rebounds the outlet to a guard on the same side of the floor.
3. The defensive team stays until their team achieves three consecutive rebounds. Players rotate offense to defense and defense out, and a new team enters on offense.

Coaching Points

- Remind players to see the player and see the ball.
- Have players block out using a reverse or forward pivot, depending on player positioning.
- Teach players to anticipate the location of the rebound.
- Remind players to be physical and make contact to hold their position.
- Remind players to focus on protection first, possession second.

Variations

- Allow the shooter to use a dribble.
- Make defensive rebounds live and the conversion into a fast break.
- Perform the drill four on four live (incorporating cross screens, down screens, screen on the ball).

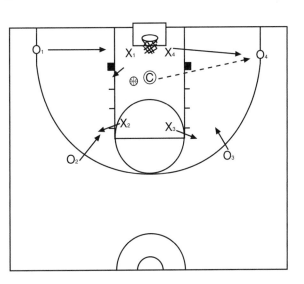

Wes Moore | *University of Tennessee at Chattanooga*

Purpose

To work on the proper technique for boxing out on rebounds and for sliding to maintain contact and inside position.

Organization

An offensive player stands just on the edge of the center circle with a defensive player facing her on the outside edge. A coach with a ball stands in the circle.

Procedure

1. The coach slaps the ball down in the center of the circle and yells "shot."
2. Player X_1 hits O_1 nose to nose and then pivots into a box-out position (see figure 1).
3. Player X_1 tries to stay low and slide along the circle line while maintaining contact with O_1 (see figure 2).
4. Player O_1 tries to get around X_1 and get the ball in the middle of the circle (see figure 3).
5. Player X_1 tries to keep O_1 away from the ball for five seconds. The coach counts out loud.

Coaching Points

- Players should initiate and maintain contact.
- Players should establish a low, wide base so that they are more difficult to get around and to move.
- Players should keep their elbows out and hands up to avoid holding calls.

Variations

Hold the ball above your head in the center circle to keep the players up rather than on the floor.

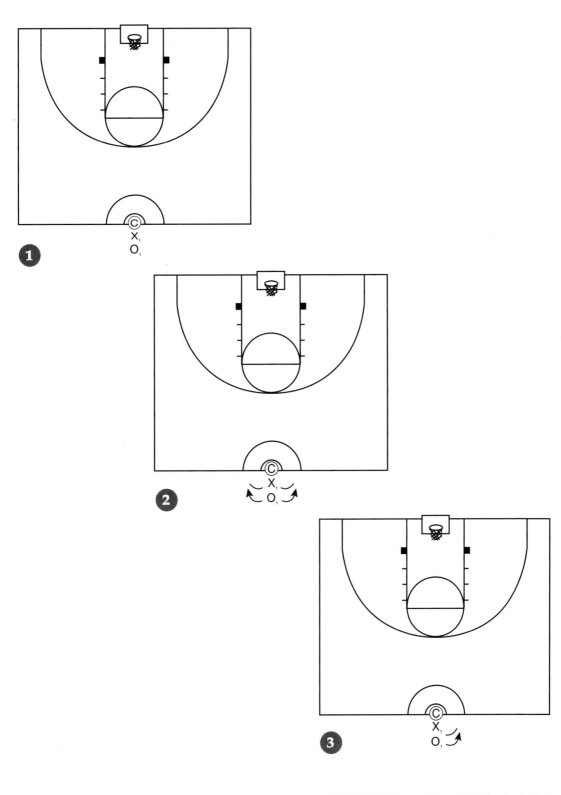

Pat Summitt | *University of Tennessee*

Purpose

To teach communication on defense and refine defensive players' reactions to the ball when offense takes a shot.

Organization

Use two defensive players, one ball, and the rest of the team in two lines of offensive players on opposite wing positions.

Procedure

1. Start on either wing; offense has the ball (see figure 1).
2. The defensive player opposite the ball calls for help.
3. The defensive player on the ball side tries to keep the ball on the sideline.
4. The offensive player can take only two dribbles, then passes across to a teammate who tries to score.
5. Defenders contest the shot, block out offensive players, and follow the shot (see figure 2).

Coaching Points

- Start with the ball in the wing player's hand. She should look to drive to the baseline.
- Allow the crosscourt pass.
- Stress both offensive and defensive rebounding.

Variation

Increase the competitiveness by starting with a pass to the wing and with the defender in denial position. Don't allow the crosscourt pass, but still challenge the offense to try it.

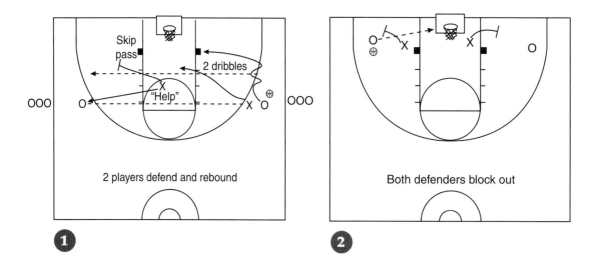

2 players defend and rebound

Both defenders block out

1   **2**

BALL IN THE MIDDLE

Laurie Kelly | *Northern Arizona University*

Purpose

To hold a block-out for an extended period.

Organization

Use one coach, one ball, one offensive player, and one defensive player at each circle on the court.

Procedure

1. The coaches set the balls on the floor in each circle.
2. Each offensive player is outside her circle and faces the ball. The defensive players face the offensive players.
3. The coach yells "shot."
4. The defense attempts to block out the offense for five seconds, keeping the offense away from the ball.
5. The defense cannot touch the ball until five seconds are up.
6. If the offense touches the ball, the defense must run.

Coaching Points

- Remind players to stay low, move their feet, and maintain balance.
- Teach players to maintain body contact and hold their positions.
- Encourage the offense to get around the block-out without fouling.

Variations

- Create teams and play for points.
- Add a second set of players and block out two on two.

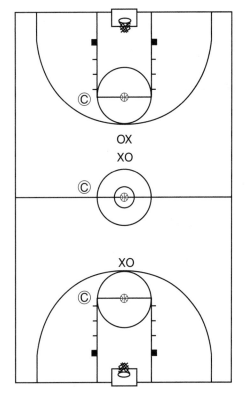

Amy Ruley | *North Dakota State University*

Purpose

To teach defending from a help position.

Organization

Use two balls and two coaches, two lines of offensive shooters and nonshooters, and one defender.

Procedure

1. The coach shoots the ball. The defender is in a help position. The offensive player crashes the boards while the defender takes one or two hard steps to meet the player to block out (see figure 1).
2. The coach makes a skip pass to an offensive player. The defender is in a help position. The defender sprints and closes out at arm's length from her player. The defender contests the shot and blocks out (see figure 2).
3. The defender blocks out nonshooters and closes out shooters consecutively for one minute.

Coaching Points

- When closing out, players should assume a defensive stance with hands high and hips low.
- When contesting a shot, defenders should keep a hand in the shooter's face and stay low when adding shot fakes.
- When blocking out, defenders should make contact and use a forward or reverse pivot depending on the player's position.
- Players should communicate and shout "shot."
- Players should maintain their balance by keeping a low center of gravity, keep their hands up, and be ready to jump and go after the ball.

Variations

- Add offensive player movement with and without the ball.
- Add another defender to work on down screens and cross screens.
- Perform the drill one on one or two on two live.

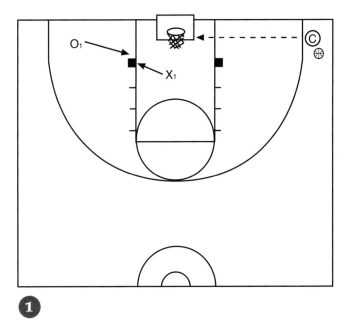

1

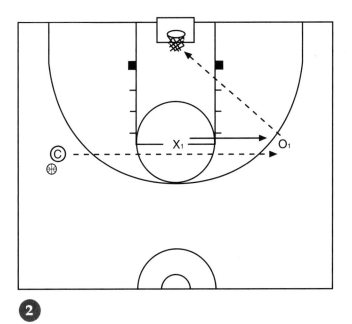

2

Laurie Kelly | *Northern Arizona University*

Purpose

To simulate half-court rebounding, encouraging the offense to crash the boards and to work on transitions from defense to offense.

Organization

Use one coach and three balls. One offensive player and two defensive players are on the court. Outlet players line up on the sideline at the free throw line extended.

Procedure

1. Player O_1 begins at the elbow, O_2 is in the outlet line, X_1 begins at the block, and X_2 begins at the opposite free throw line.
2. The coach starts with a ball at the other elbow and calls "shot."
3. Player O_1 crashes the boards and X_1 blocks out.
4. The coach shoots after calling shot to provide realistic timing for the block-out and crashing (see figure 1).
5. Player X_1 rebounds the ball, pivots outside and passes to O_2, who has come off the outlet line (see figure 2).
6. Players X_1 and O_2 play two on one against the X_2 on the other end (see figure 3).
7. Player X_1 goes to the outlet line, O_2 goes to defense under the opposite goal, and X_2 goes to block-out line.
8. After all players have played each position, they perform the drill on the other side of the basket.
9. If the offense rebounds the ball, they try to score. If the offense scores, the same defense goes again.

Coaching Points

- Demand body contact by the defense on every possession.
- Challenge the offense to get around the block-out without fouling.
- Remind players to find their player, hit their player, and go get the ball.
- Teach players to keep the ball high on the rebound and locate their outlet pass.
- Have players sprint up the floor after rebounding the ball.

Variations

- Players pressure the outlet passer and defend the outlet.
- Defenders who give up offensive rebounds must sprint.

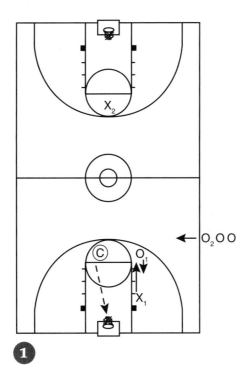

1

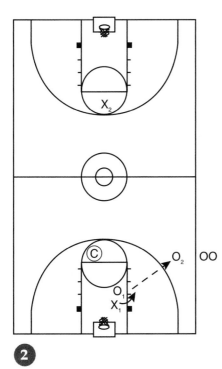

2

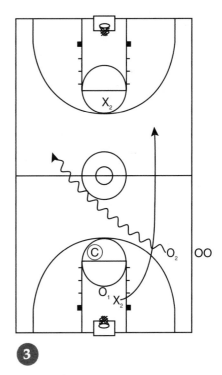

3

Laurie Kelly | Northern Arizona University

Purpose

To simulate a game situation of half-court rebounding, while encouraging the offense to crash the boards. To simulate the physicality of rebounding in traffic.

Organization

Use three coaches or managers and two balls. Two offensive players are on the court with two offensive lines outside the three-point line. Two defensive players are on the court with two defensive lines under the goal. Use a rebound ring to create realistic missed shots.

Procedure

1. The coach starts with a ball at the free throw line. Managers start at the free throw line extended in the outlet pass position. One manager has a ball. The offense starts on each elbow. The defense starts on each block.
2. The coach calls "shot" to cue the offense to crash the boards and the defense to block out. The coach then shoots to provide realistic timing for the block-out and crashing.
3. The defense must block out the offensive player at the opposite elbow (see figure 1).
4. After gaining possession of the rebound, the rebounder passes to the manager as outlet.
5. The coach continues to shoot for two minutes, getting balls from the manager receiving the outlet passes (see figure 2).
6. Each defensive player rotates to the opposite defensive line. Each offensive player rotates to the opposite offensive line.
7. After two minutes, the teams switch from offense to defense.
8. Offensive rebounds are worth two points. Defensive rebounds are worth one point.
9. The team with the most points wins.

Coaching Points

- Demand body contact by the defense on every possession.
- Demand that the offense get around the block-out without fouling.
- Remind players to find their player, hit their player, and go get the ball.
- Teach players to track the ball as they block out and that most misses go to the weak side.

Variations

- Start the drill from a wing position and locate the players in denial and help-side defensive positions for each side of the floor.
- Shoot three-pointers to create longer rebounds.

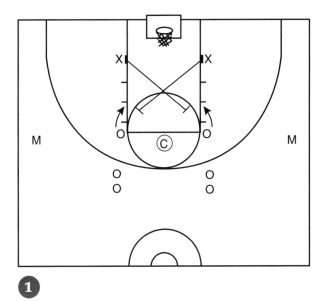

1

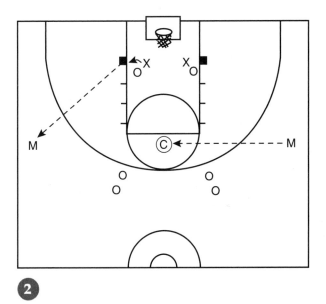

2

SCRAMBLE REBOUNDING

Laurie Kelly | *Northern Arizona University*

Purpose
To simulate half-court rebounding out of a rotation or scramble situation.

Organization
Use two coaches, three offensive players, three defensive players, and one ball.

Procedure
1. The coaches start on either end of the free throw line extended. One coach has a ball.
2. The offense begins at the top of the key and at each corner.
3. The defensive players stand in front of offensive players and keep one foot in the lane.
4. The coaches pass the ball back and forth as the defenders rotate positions on each pass (see figure 1).
5. The coaches shoot randomly as the defense shifts positions. The defense calls out "shot."
6. Each defender blocks out the player in front of her.
7. The offense crashes the boards (see figure 2).
8. The defense rebounds the ball, pivots outside, and makes an outlet pass to a coach (see figure 3).
9. The defense moves to offense if they get a rebound.
10. If the offense rebounds the ball, offense outlets, and a new defense rotates on. New teams always rotate in on defense.
11. Continue the drill for 5 to 10 minutes. Defensive rebounds earn two points. Offensive rebounds earn one point. The team with the most points wins.

Coaching Points
- Players should communicate on each pass to make sure rotations are happening and everyone is blocked out.
- Defenders should make body contact on every possession.
- The offense should get around the block out without fouling.
- Players must find their player, hit their player, and go get the ball.
- Players should keep the ball high on the rebound and locate their outlet pass.

Variations
- Change the point system to give more reward for offense.
- Change positioning on the court to realistic denial and helpside positions.
- Go four on four or five on five.

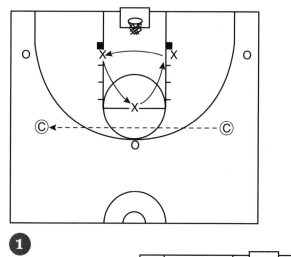

1

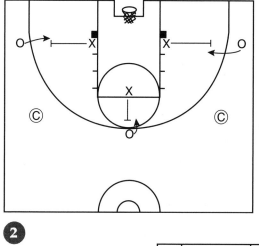

2

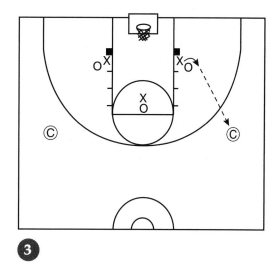

3

OUTLET REBOUNDING

Trina Patterson | *University of Albany*

Purpose
To develop good ballhandling, passing, and rebounding skills.

Organization
Half the team forms a rebound line under the basket; each has a ball. A partner for each player is at the three-point line as an outlet.

Procedure
1. The rebounder tosses the ball off the backboard and retrieves it.
2. The outlet player calls "outlet" and steps to receive a pass then squares up to face up the floor.
3. The rebounder passes to the outlet player and fills the right lane, calling "right."
4. The outlet player dribbles the ball to the middle of the floor and slightly to the left.
5. The outlet player delivers a pass to the rebounder, who is cutting hard for a layup.
6. The passer rebounds; the shooter becomes the outlet player on the return trip to the opposite end of the court.

Coaching Points
- The rebounder should go after the rebound with two hands, keeping the ball high.
- The rebounder pivots toward the outside and throws an overhead pass.

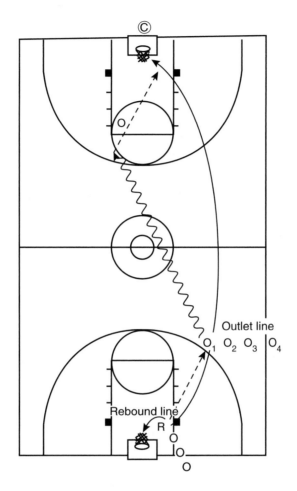

Outlet line

O_1 O_2 O_3 O_4

Rebound line

R

O

O

O

chapter 13

Defensive Transition Drills

With today's game being fast paced and transition oriented, it's no wonder coaches are looking at defensive transition a little differently than they did 15 years ago. Isn't transition on defense just about getting back and stopping the ball? Well, mostly yes, but in this chapter you'll learn how the top coaches teach their players not only to get back and stop the ball, but also to attempt to dictate and control the offensive team's efforts from the point of turnover.

Essentially, coaches aren't satisfied with just getting back; many attempt to control the offensive tempo (sometimes in the backcourt off the rebound) and cause the ball to turn over again before assuming they are back on defense. Still, there are plenty of teams who rely on sprinting back and protecting the paint. Read on and you'll learn how top coaches approach this aspect of the game. Perhaps you'll see some virtue in building their ideas into your winning strategies.

TRANSITION D: ONE-ON-ONE

Jane Albright | Wichita State University

Purpose

To make the offensive player turn or change directions and work on full-court one-on-one defense.

Organization

Players pair up by size and speed, and then line up on the baseline, each pair with a ball.

Procedure

1. Both players start at the baseline.
2. The defender (X) slides to the manager at the hash mark and slaps the manager's hand.
3. The offensive player waits until the defender gets to the manager before starting to dribble.
4. The defender tries to sprint to half-court to meet the offensive player, who is trying to score at the opposite end of the court.

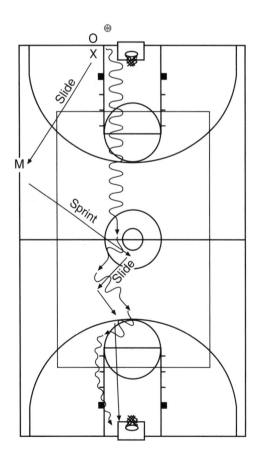

5. The defender tries to slow the offense by forcing her to change the direction of her dribble.
6. Players go one on one at the opposite end until the offensive player scores or the defender gets a rebound or steal.

Coaching Point

Emphasize staying low on the slide, sprinting hard, and working to make the offensive player change directions with her dribble. This will slow her down and make her easier to defend.

CATCH-UP

Muffet McGraw | *University of Notre Dame*

Purpose

To work on transition defense while allowing the offense to work on a three-on-two situation.

Organization

Three defenders are along the free throw line, and three offensive players are on the baseline. The coach has the ball.

Procedure

1. The coach throws the ball to any of the three offensive players on the baseline.
2. Whoever has lined up to defend the player with the ball runs and touches the baseline while the offense takes off three on two.
3. The third defender sprints to catch up, then plays three on three.

Coaching Points

- The defense should form a tandem until the third defender arrives.
- The top player stops the penetration and forces a pass.
- The bottom defender goes out to defend the first pass off the key.
- The last defender down picks up whoever is at the top.

Variations

- Play it out three on three, and come back down the court three on three against full-court pressure.
- Instead of touching the baseline, the defender can take off once the ball has passed her.

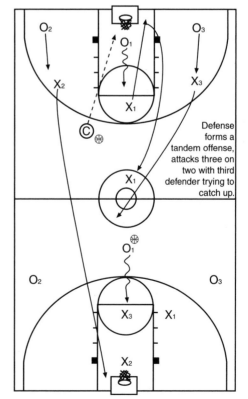

Defense forms a tandem offense, attacks three on two with third defender trying to catch up.

Gary Blair | *Texas A&M University*

Purpose

To simulate transition defense and to teach good offensive spacing and two-on-two play.

Organization

Divide the team into two groups: offense and defense. The coach needs two balls to keep the drill moving.

Procedure

1. Four offensive team members space out along the same sideline, baseline to baseline.
2. Two defensive team members start at the free throw lane lines, opposite each other.
3. The coach initiates the drill with a toss to O_1. On the toss, X_1 and X_2 sprint to defend O_3 and O_4 (see figure 1).
4. Player O_1 passes to O_2, who passes to O_3, who passes to O_4. Players O_4 and O_3 then go live against X_1 and X_2.
5. They play two on two until the offense scores or the defense stops them. Everyone goes off around the outside of the court to the end of lines they started in (see figure 2).
6. The next two defenders in line become X_1 and X_2. Players O_1 and O_2 rotate to the O_3 and O_4 spots, and the next two in the offensive line step into O_1 and O_2. The coach tosses the ball to O_1 and repeats the drill.

Coaching Points

- The offense must make strong, quick, crisp passes.
- The defense must sprint to get into defensive position.
- Each group plays offense for a certain number of minutes, then switches.

Variation

Keep score to make this a fun, competitive drill that improves conditioning without players realizing it.

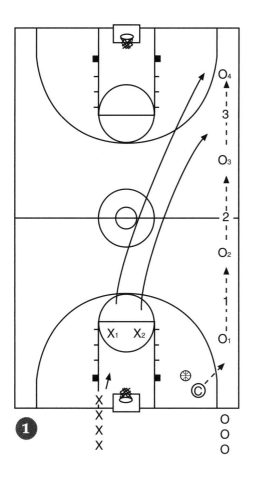

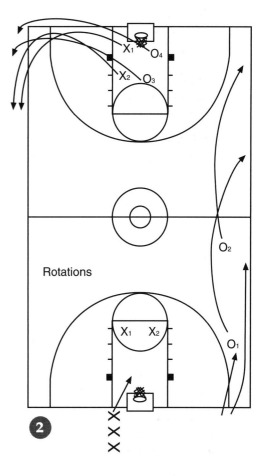

Rotations

Wendy Larry | *Old Dominion University*

Purpose

To improve defensive communication and teamwork against a fast break. This is also an excellent conditioning drill.

Organization

Use two teams and one ball. One team lines up on a hash mark. The other team lines up at the hash mark on the opposite side and other half of the court. Run the clock for five to seven minutes.

Procedure

1. Three players from each team step onto the court. The three that are on their own side of the floor are on defense.
2. These players play three on three until the offense scores or the defense gets the ball by rebounding or stealing.
3. If the offense scores or defense gets the ball, the defense becomes offense.
4. The defender who steals or rebounds (on a make or a miss) outlets the ball to her teammate who is next in line, then goes to the end of the line (see figure 1).
5. The outlet and two other defenders attack the three offensive players on a three-on-three fast break (see figure 2).
6. Repeat steps two through five until time runs out.

Coaching Points

- Players will get tired quickly; don't let them get lazy and stop doing the little things.
- The outlet must receive the ball below the foul line extended. You'll have one-on-none breaks if you allow them to receive farther up the court.
- Keep score. The losing team runs sprints after the drill is over.
- If the ball goes out of bounds, give the ball to the team who hustles to get the ball.

Variations

- Set the clock for a different amount of time.
- Give points for things other than a basket, for example, an offensive rebound, a good box-out, a steal, or a hustle.

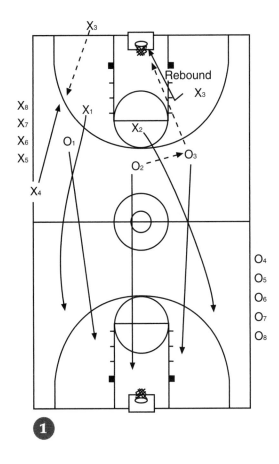

Rebound

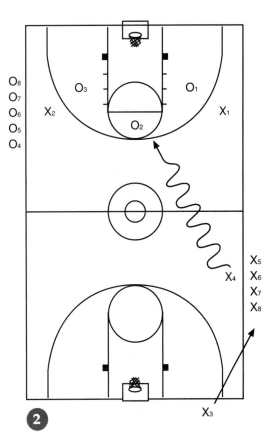

Tim Shea | *Salem State College*

Purpose

To improve communication, to prevent open shots, and to learn to rotate to the open player.

Organization

Divide players into teams of three with different colored shirts on half a court. One team is on offense with the ball, and one team is on defense. The remaining teams are under the basket.

Procedure

1. The teams play three on three until one team scores.
2. The team that gives up the score leaves the court quickly while the next team on the baseline rushes onto the court to identify whom to defend.
3. The scoring team does not wait for the new team to get into good defensive position, but gets the ball quickly, clears it behind the three-point line, passes it in, and plays.
4. After a score, only the offensive team may grab the ball.

Coaching Points

- The winning team is the first one to make 10 baskets. If done correctly, the losing teams will be too exhausted for much more than a token penalty sprint.
- Treat a foul the same as a score.
- If two teams have had a few chances on offense, chase both off the court and bring on the next two teams.
- Your emphasis should be on the team rushing onto the court. Team members need to talk, point, identify perimeter shooters, and defend them accordingly.

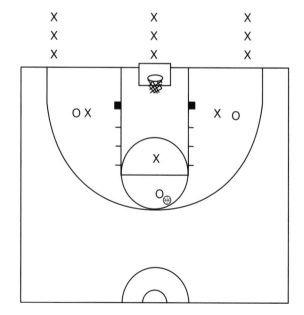

Variation

Play four-on-four-on-four.

VT RELEASE

Bonnie Henrickson | *University of Kansas*

Purpose

To emphasize the fullback position (the player assigned to protect the basket) in defensive transition.

Organization

Use six offensive players, five defensive players, and one ball.

Procedure

1. Five players execute the coach's offense or freelance, depending on what the coach wants.
2. On the coach's command, a player takes a shot.
3. The rebounder outlets to the point guard and goes out of the drill to make it five on five on the other end.
4. Player O_6 releases (flies) on your command to force the fullback to get back on the shot.
5. In the figure, O_1 is the fullback, and O_2 stops the ball.

Coaching Points

- Let the outlet throw the ball to the players flying, if they are open.
- Stop to check the defensive position of all five players.

Variations

- Start this drill with four on four and build to five on five.
- Use a rebound ring on the basket when playing five on five to work on rebounding.
- Establish a time limit for the shot attempt.

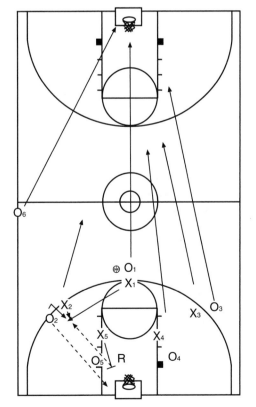

OLYMPIC DEFENSE

Tim Shea | *Salem State College*

Purpose

To teach communication, to learn how to play help defense, and to learn how to recover on defense.

Organization

Three offensive players are on the end line, facing the coach. Three defensive players are at the free throw line, facing the offensive players. The coach has the ball at the free throw line (see figure 1).

Procedure

1. The coach passes the ball to any offensive player on the end line. The three offensive players break down the court.
2. The defender facing the player who received the pass sprints to the end line and touches it while her two teammates run down the court and into the paint (see figure 2). Player X_1 calls "ball" when she is within 15 feet (4.5 meters) of the basket. Player X_3 positions herself in the low post area.
3. After touching the end line, X_1 determines where she is most needed while sprinting back.
4. Players X_2 and X_3 try to force as many passes as possible while protecting the basket and awaiting the help of X_1.
5. Play continues until the offense scores or is stopped.
6. Teams switch (offense to defense) to return down the court to repeat the same setup.

Coaching Point

Avoid colliding with the ball and players.

Variation

Allow one of the retreating defenders to gamble by not going all the way down the court immediately.

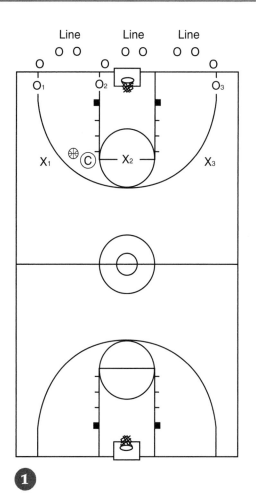

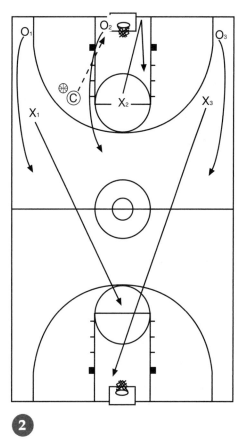

1

2

TWO-ON-TWO FULL:
DEFENDING ON-BALL SCREENS

Beth Burns | San Diego State University

Purpose

To work defending using on-ball screens to counter full court and half-court pressure and inbounding the ball against pressure.

Organization

Divide the team into groups of four (two pairs, each pair with one guard and one forward). Use one ball per group of four.

Procedure

1. All four players are on the court. The coach shoots and makes a layup.
2. Player O_2 gets the ball out of the net, clears the paint, and inbounds to O_1. Player O_1 breaks to an outlet. Player X_2 pressures a pass, and X_1 forces an outlet to the ball (see figure 1).
3. Player O_1 turns up the court, and O_2 sets the on-ball screen. The offense sets at least one screen in the backcourt (see figure 2).
4. O_2 sets another screen on or around the three-point line of the frontcourt (see figure 3).
5. Offense attacks the basket to score after the second screen.
6. If offense makes the basket, X_2 clears the paint and inbounds. Players O_1 and O_2 must react and match up. Player X_2 sets the on-ball screens.
7. If the missed shot goes to the defense, O_1 and O_2 must react and match up. Defense sets the on-ball screens.

Coaching Points

- In the backcourt, X_1 has on-ball pressure, and X_2 stays 12 to 15 feet (3.7 to 4.6 meters) deeper than the ball, talking loud, "Pick coming." Keep X_2's head on the line of the ball (moving laterally, not forward). Player X_1 slides behind the screen, and then meets the ball on the other side. Players repeat this process on any on-ball screen in the backcourt.
- At the three-point line, players foot to foot and go over with no switch. The forward stays with the ball until the guard recovers. Defense hears the screen and forces the ball to X_2; X_2 steps toward the ball (not laterally or behind), keeping her inside hand on O_2's hip. If the hip leaves, X_2 leaves because there is no longer a screen (see figure 4). The goal is to force the ball wide or back with no middle penetration.

Variation

Players can trap on the on-ball screen.

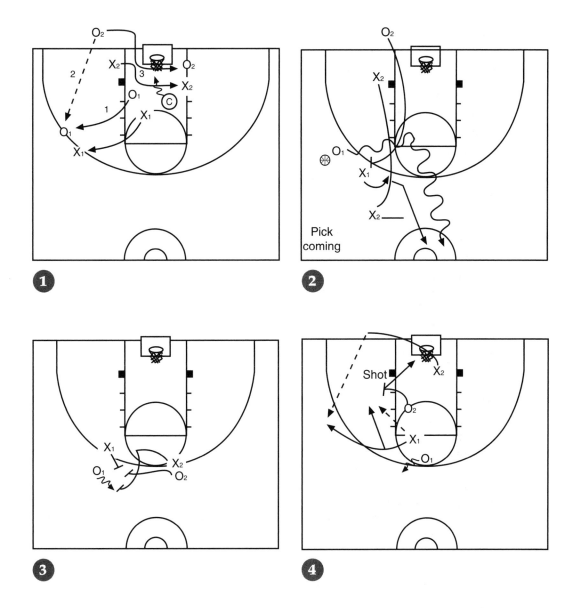

1

2

Pick
coming

3

4

Shot

Beth Burns | San Diego State University

Purpose

To teach transition defense, rebounding, defensive positioning, and switching on screens.

Organization

Use two offensive and two defensive players and one ball per group of four. Pair players of similar size, speed, and ability; use a rebound ring to create rebound opportunities.

Procedure

1. Player X_1 starts with the ball near the baseline and gives it to O_1. Her partner, X_2, is in help position (she may or may not be in denial). See figure 1.
2. Player O_1 penetrates in straight lines; O_2 can sprint out to spread over the floor.
3. As X_1 pressures, O_2 sets the on-ball screen. Player X_2 reacts and calls "switch."
4. The offense takes a shot, but can only get the point by getting the offensive rebound (see figure 2).
5. When X_1 or X_2 gets possession, she transitions to the other end. Players O_1 and O_2 immediately stop the ball and match up. Players X_1 and X_2 must score (no rebound ring on this basket) to get points.

Coaching Points

- Don't be surprised if the defense gets beat early. This drill forces two players to communicate to be successful.
- Do foot on foot on all switches. Encourage offense to split the screen (ball handler) or slip the screen (screener).
- Use a basket cover-up to make the offense go hard to the glass to score; this makes stopping the transition a challenge.
- Emphasize communication and conditioning.
- Have players take turns getting the ball first.
- Go four to six minutes with three groups of four; the winners are those who get the most points.

Variation

Depending on your goal, you can have at least two on-ball screens or just one screen if pressure dictates it.

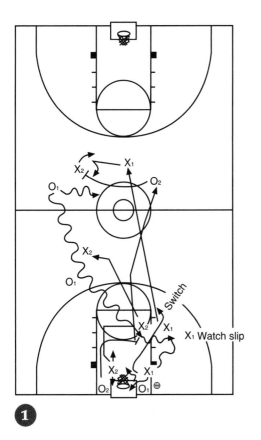

Switch

X₁ Watch slip

1

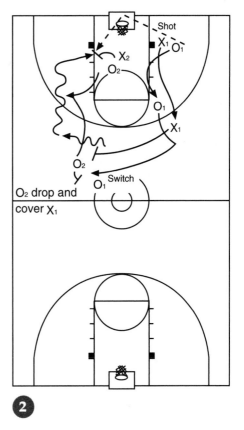

Shot

Switch

O₂ drop and
cover X₁

2

Beth Burns | *San Diego State University*

Purpose

To play full-court on-ball defense; to focus on conditioning.

Organization

Pair up players, and give each pair one ball. Use the 30-second shot clock.

Procedure

1. Player X_1 has the ball and starts with her head under the net and her feet set to force the drive to the weak hand. She hands the ball to the O_1.
2. The offensive player tries to attack in straight lines; in the backcourt, X_1 turns the offensive player as many times as possible.
3. As the ball approaches half-court, the defense should cut the floor and keep the ball on one side.
4. Defense contests the shot and boxes out.
5. Partners jog back as the next pair starts. The coach calls the shot clock.

Coaching Points

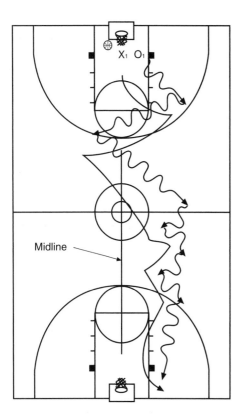

- Players should use aggression with intelligence.
- The defensive player should always have one hand in front of the offensive player's eyes to obscure her vision and prevent a full-court pass.
- Players should force as many turns as possible in the backcourt.
- Players should make constant chatter, "ball, ball, ball."
- If the offense hesitates, the defensive player should say "jump back" and then jump back at least the length of the offensive player's first step. She should keep the hands up to block a full-court pass.
- The defensive player should cut the floor in half, allowing no middle penetration.
- The defensive player should contest the shot, box out, and play to finish. Call fouls.
- Reward the defense if 21 seconds or fewer are left on the clock. This means the defense forced lots of turns and applied good pressure. If 26 or 27 seconds remain, the ball came up the court too quickly.
- Winners get a drink while the losers do push-ups.
- The drill lasts four minutes for a team of twelve players.

THREE-ON-TWO PLUS ONE

Bonnie Henrickson | *University of Kansas*

Purpose

To learn the concept of a tandem defensive set; to learn how to stop penetration and protect the basket on defense, even when outnumbered.

Organization

Use three offensive players, three defensive players, one coach, and one ball.

Procedure

1. Three offensive players line up on the baseline; three defensive players are on the free throw line (see figure 1).
2. The coach throws the ball to any offensive player.
3. The defensive player standing across from the receiver sprints to touch the baseline, which she is facing.
4. Players X_2 and X_3 sprint back and get into a tandem defensive position. Player X_2 takes the first pass, and X_3 drops to the baseline. Player X_1 sprints back to guard O_2 (see figure 2).

Coaching Points

- Make sure X_3 drops below O_3 and is at basket level for help.
- Emphasize communication.

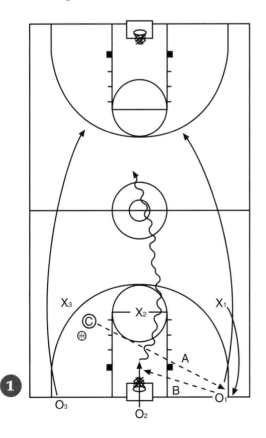

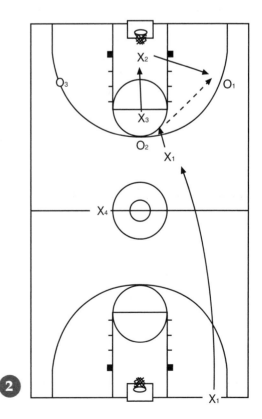

FIVE-ON-FOUR PLUS ONE

Bonnie Henrickson | *University of Kansas*

Purpose

To learn how to stop the ball in transition and communicate rotations once the ball gets to half-court.

Organization

Use five offensive players, five defensive players, and one ball.

Procedure

1. The five offensive players line up on the baseline; the five defensive players line up on the free throw line extended (see figure 13.10*a*).
2. The coach throws the ball to an offensive player. The defensive player standing across from the receiver runs to touch the baseline she's facing.
3. Ahead of time, the coach has dictated which defender will stop the ball and which defender will protect the basket. Player X_1 protects the basket, and X_2 stops the ball (see figure 1).
4. Player X_4 sprints the length of the floor to make it five on five (see figure 2).
5. The offense tries to get a high-percentage shot before it becomes five on five.

Coaching Points

- Stop play opposite the three-point line to check the defensive positions.
- Emphasize communication—players must talk and find their matchups.
- Have the defense line up in positions other than posts across from posts and guards across from guards. This gives you mismatches.

Variation

Establish a time limit for scoring (e.g., the offense has to take a shot in 12 seconds).

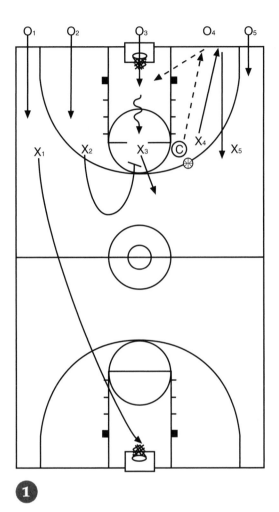

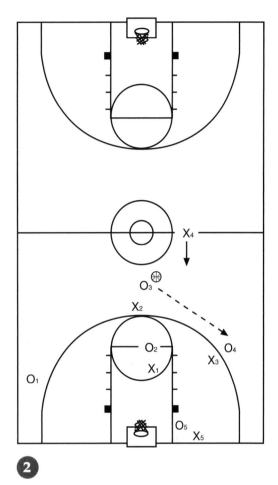

1

2

Rene Portland | *Penn State University*

Purpose

To work on players' ballhandling skills while also improving players' defensive skills and stamina.

Organization

Two offensive players, each with a ball, and one defensive player start on the baseline.

Procedure

1. The defensive player steps onto the court (see figure 1).
2. Player O_1 attempts to beat the defensive player to half-court using a variety of dribbles.
3. The defensive player attempts to contain the offensive player by forcing her to change direction.
4. Once both players reach half-court, the defensive player sprints back toward the basket. Player O_2 calls out a shot (layup, elbow, three-pointer) and passes a ball to the former defensive player. The player catches the ball and shoots the shot that was called. Player O_1 goes back to the baseline (see figure 2).
5. After player X shoots, she plays defense on the next person in line. The defensive player goes three times, executing each shot listed in number 4.

Coaching Point

This is challenging for the defensive player. She will need plenty of encouragement to survive the drill.

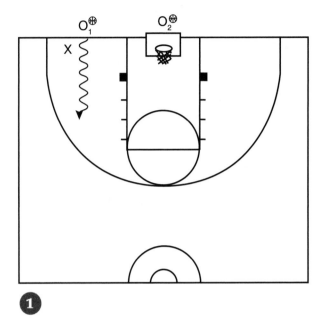

1

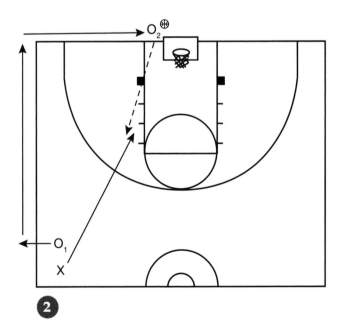

2

chapter 14

Perimeter Drills

The pressure from a team like Tennessee or Rutgers might give some coaches or players nightmares. And the players on those teams know they have worked long and hard to make their opponents' nights sleepless. The hard work, unselfishness, and effort that go into applying full-court unrelenting perimeter pressure are remarkable. Not many players, much less entire teams, can make that kind of commitment successfully over time.

Nonetheless, unrelenting full-court perimeter pressure is the cornerstone of many championship teams. The fear they impose is the result of confidence and total team commitment, the knowledge that everyone will sacrifice to make the play or control the tempo. Many of these teams are made up of average to above-average players with extraordinary enthusiasm and commitment to unselfish play.

Regardless of your defensive philosophy, do your players know how to deny entry passes, cut cutters, and influence dribblers? If you'd like help reinforcing their skills, refocusing their abilities, or pushing their limits, read on to see what some of the best coaches in the country are doing to make sure their players are sleeping soundly at night.

DOUBLING ON-BALL SCREENS

Elaine Elliott | University of Utah

Purpose
To improve players' footwork and ability to double on-ball screens.

Organization
Use four players (two offensive and two defensive), one coach, and one ball.

Procedure
1. Player O_1 starts with the ball on the right wing. Player O_2 starts at the block with defense. The coach is at the top of the key.
2. Player O_2 comes out and sets an on-ball screen on the sideline side of X_1.
3. When the screen is set, X_1 immediately shifts to force O_1 to her right to use the screen. Player X_1 should prevent O_1 from dribbling to the middle of the court. Player X_2 moves above O_2, into a hedge position, to prevent O_1 from coming off O_2's screen. Player X_2 should be close enough to O_2 that their feet are either touching or overlapping a little (see figure 1).
4. Player O_1 tries to dribble to the basket, either to the left or to the right. Player X_1 and X_2 should prevent this by closing in on player O_1 so that her only options are to back dribble or to pick up the ball (see figure 2).
5. The drill ends when player O_1 is able to beat the trap and get to the basket or when player O_1 picks up the ball. When a dead ball occurs, defenders close in and prevent a pass out of double team. Players go until there is a pass to the coach or a dead-ball five-second count.

Coaching Points
- Defenders must keep their knees bent and seat down and shuffle their feet when trapping. They should not reach to get the ball.
- The defenders' priority should be to prevent being split by the offensive player. They also should prevent the offensive player from getting to the middle of the court by forcing her into the sideline.

Variations
- Players perform this drill on both sides of the floor and on both ends if there are enough players.
- Player O_1 may be a coach in order to control the offensive movement. For example, the coach takes only four or five back dribbles, then picks up for a dead ball.

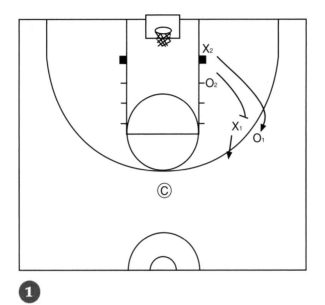

1

2

ON-BALL AND OFF-BALL DEFENSE

Elaine Elliott | *University of Utah*

Purpose
To teach defenders on-ball and off-ball defensive positions.

Organization
Use two offensive players, two defensive players, two coaches, one ball, and a 30-second shot clock.

Procedure
1. One offensive player is at each wing position. Two coaches are at the top of the key with a ball. One defender is on each offensive wing player.
2. The defense is positioned according to where the ball begins. The ball is with the left coach (see figure 1). Therefore, the left wing defense is one pass away in deny stance. The other defender is two passes away, so she should be in an open pistol stance, one foot in the lane and pointing to see both her player and the ball.
3. The defense shifts position when the offense passes the ball. If the ball is passed to the right coach, X_1 moves into an open stance with one foot in the lane because she is now two passes away. Player X_2 sprints into a denial stance on her offensive player because she is one pass away (see figure 2).
4. If offense then passes the ball to O_2, the defender moves from denial to an on-ball stance. The other defender sprints to the middle of the lane, still in pistol stance (see figure 3).
5. The offense passes the ball around the perimeter for the duration of the 30-second shot clock.

Coaching Points
- Defenders should move when the ball is in the air, not after the pass has been made.
- Defenders must stay low in their stances and be able to see their players and the ball.
- Offensive players and managers should hold the ball for a few seconds so the defense can adjust.

Variations
- Have offensive players drive to the basket or shoot on the catch. Have defenders prevent the drive or contest the shot, block out, and rebound.
- Add skip passes for defensive closeout work.
- Add more time to the drill for conditioning.

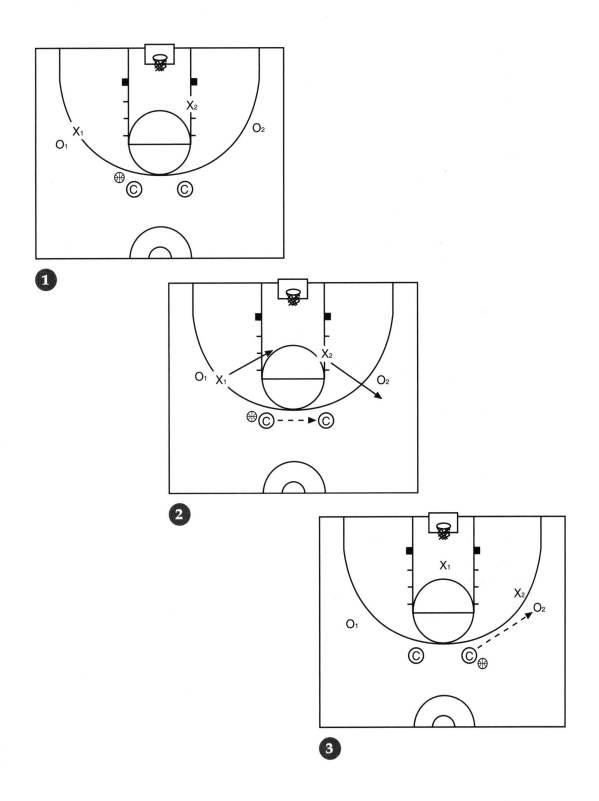

HELP AND RECOVER

Nancy Fahey | *Washington University*

Purpose

To work on help-and-recover out of a three-player half-court weave.

Organization

Divide players into groups of three offensive players, each with a ball.

Procedure

1. Players form three lines at half-court with the basketball in the middle. The drill can be run on both half-courts at the same time.
2. Player O_1 passes the ball to O_2 and cuts behind O_2 as she dribbles to the free throw line area. Player O_3 sprints to the lane and gets into a defensive stance (see figure 1).
3. Player O_2 passes the ball to player O_1 at the wing. Player O_3 closes out on O_1, who has the ball. Once O_3 has closed out, O_1 drives the ball hard to the baseline. Player O_3 must not give up the baseline drive (see figure 2).
4. Once the ball is stopped, O_3 yells "dead" to alert her teammates that the ball handler has given up her dribble. Player O_1 then passes the ball to O_2 at the free throw lane area. Player O_3 again must close out.
5. Players O_2 and O_3 play one on one. The drill stops when the offense has scored or the defense secures a rebound or gets a steal.

Coaching Points

- Players should focus on closeout footwork.
- Players should stop the baseline drive.
- Players should not give up a layup in either position.

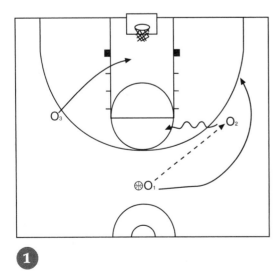

1

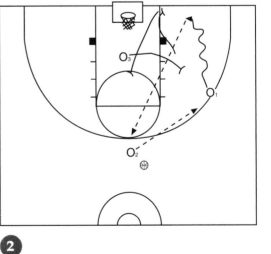

2

157   DEFENSIVE KNOCKDOWN

Nancy Fahey | *Washington University*

Purpose

To reinforce wing denial defense with four or five quick repetitions against offense.

Organization

Use one offensive player, one defensive player, one coach, one manager, and four or five balls.

Procedure

1. Player O_1 starts at the wing. Player X_1 takes a denial defensive stance.
2. The coach has two basketballs, and the manager is standing next to the coach, with two or three additional basketballs ready to pass to the coach. The coach is on one knee, ready to toss the first ball. The remaining players retrieve the basketballs as the defense knocks the basketballs away (see figure 1).
3. The coach bounces the ball to start the drill. On the bounce, O_1 starts backdoor and pops back out to the wing. Player X_1 slides down and back to the wing. On a toss from the coach, X_1 knocks the ball down using correct footwork and correct hand movements.
4. Player O_1 makes three or four cuts; X_1 knocks the ball down each time. On the fourth ball, O_1 cuts to the opposite wing. The coach passes the ball to O_1 at the opposite wing. Players O_1 and X_1 play one on one until O_1 scores or X_1 secures the ball on a steal or rebound (see figure 2).

Coaching Points

- Players should use appropriate footwork, and the denial hand should have the palm toward the coach.
- Players should knock the ball rather than turning to catch it.

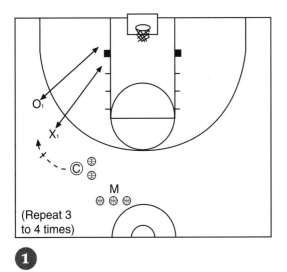

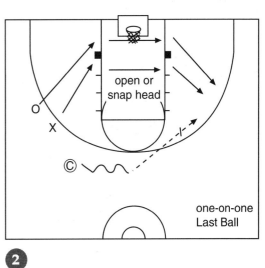

CUTTING LOOSE

Theresa Grentz | *University of Illinois*

Purpose
To improve defensive post play.

Organization
Use one offensive player, one defensive player, and one coach.

Procedure
1. Each offensive and defensive player begins the drill at the top of the key.
2. The coach takes a position in the wing area on the same side of the floor.
3. The drill begins with the offensive player passing the ball to the coach, then cutting down the lane for the return pass from the coach. The offensive player makes cuts within the lane in an attempt to get open.
4. The defensive player must defend all cuts by the offense.

Coaching Points
- The defense must decide whether to front, play ballside defense, or overplay pressure on the ball side.
- Players should focus on maintaining correct position on defense in the post.

Variation
Add weakside help for defensive players.

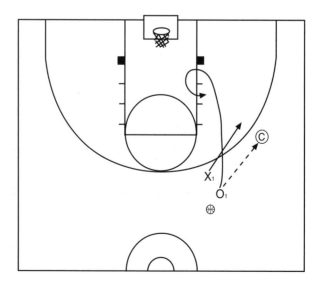

SHELL DEFENSE

Theresa Grentz | *University of Illinois*

Purpose

To teach basic perimeter defense.

Organization

Two offensive players are on either side of the top of the key, and offensive players are in both low wing areas. Four defensive players match up accordingly.

Procedure

1. Either guard may start with the ball. The defensive player pressures the ball.
2. Players that are one pass away from the ball maintain one hand in the passing lane at all times.
3. The offense moves to present the best possible passing target.
4. As the ball changes position, the defensive players adjust their positions accordingly.

Coaching Points

- The player guarding the ball always applies pressure to minimize the offense's ability to see the passing lanes.
- The defensive players who are one pass away should deny the pass.
- The defender who is more than one pass away should be prepared to help on penetration to the basket.
- Players should see both the ball and their offensive player at all times.

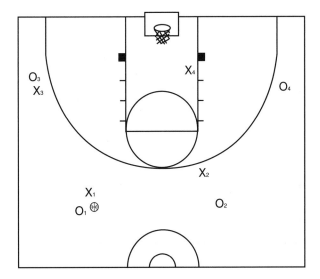

TIMED SHELL

Kris Huffman | DePauw University

Purpose

To help establish team defensive concepts. This drill works on ballside and helpside hedging and moving with each pass and finishes with a rebound.

Organization

Four offensive players and four defensive players line up around the three-point line. One of the offensive players has the ball. The remaining players form four lines behind the offensive players. A manager times the drill.

Procedure

1. Any offensive player may start with the ball. Defenders assume proper positions.
2. The offense passes the ball around the perimeter; the defense adjusts with each pass.
3. The manager blows the whistle after 20 seconds. Offense becomes defense, and defense chooses a different line.
4. After each player has played defense for one or two sequences, dribble penetration is added to the drill.
5. The defense must help and recover. The offense tries to score.
6. The defense stays on the floor for 20 seconds before rotating.

Coaching Points

- The player guarding the ball should apply pressure.
- Defensive players one pass away should deny; defenders two passes away should be in the helpside position.
- On the penetration, the defense should see the ball and stop the ball.

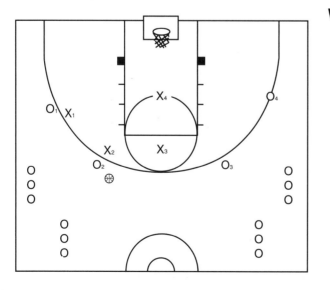

Variations

- Add the give-and-go option to make the defense work on jumping to the ball.
- Add the weakside flash.
- Have all the defenders begin in the lane, and pass the ball to any offensive player. The defense must quickly establish a good defensive position relative to the ball.

ONE-ON-ONE FORCE CORNER

Kris Huffman | DePauw University

Purpose

To force the offense to the corner by keeping the ball out of the middle of the floor and to prevent ball reversal.

Organization

Offensive players form a line at one wing, one player defends, and a coach with the ball is at the other wing.

Procedure

1. The drill begins with a skip pass from the coach to the first offensive player in the line.
2. The defender adjusts from help side to defending the ball with a good close-out.
3. The drill is now one on one.
4. The defender attempts to force the ball to the corner and to protect the middle.
5. The drill ends with a basket or the rebound and outlet pass.

Coaching Points

- The defender must close out in a stance with the inside foot and hand up.
- The defender must not give up an open lane to the basket when trying to keep the offensive player out of the middle. The feet should be angled to the corner, not the baseline.

Variation

Limit the number of dribbles allowed by the offense.

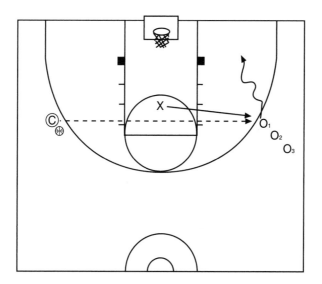

Wendy Larry | *Old Dominion University*

Purpose

To practice perimeter defensive positioning when a player is one pass away and denying the ball. This drill also works on helpside positioning when the ball is on the opposite side of the court.

Organization

Position one offensive and one defensive player on each wing. Two coaches are at the top of the key; one has a ball.

Procedure

1. One coach starts with the ball. The offensive player on this side attempts to get open while the defense denies.
2. The off-ball defensive player is two passes away and should be in a help position.
3. If the offensive player gets open and receives the ball, the players play two on two until the offense scores or the defense gets the ball.
4. If the offensive player on that side of the court cannot get open, one coach passes to the other coach, and they repeat steps 1 through 3.
5. If the defense successfully denies the offense the ball four times in a row, the offense switches to defense.

Coaching Points

- If the defense is doing a great job of denying, try to get a pass through. Let them get a deflection so they realize the benefits of denying properly.
- Remind the defense to use the proper hand to deflect while denying. Players should maintain proper spacing. The defender should not set up too close to the offensive player.
- Allow the offense to make a backdoor cut. Off-ball help should be there.

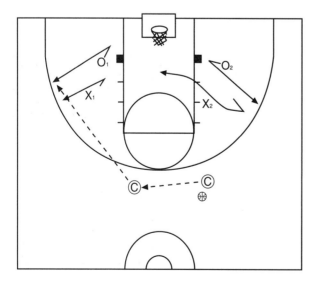

Variations

- To keep the drill moving quickly, require only two good denials, or if the offense scores, the defense moves off.
- If you have more than four at the basket, rotate players in and out.

THREE-PLAYER HELP AND RECOVER

Pat Summitt | *University of Tennessee*

Purpose

To teach ball pressure and helpside recovery.

Organization

Use three lines of players, three offensive players, three defensive players, and one ball.

Procedure

1. Players start at one end of the floor with the ball in the middle line.
2. The player with the ball can dribble twice, then must pass to either wing.
3. The wing player dribbles twice and passes to the middle or skips to the wing.
4. The first time through, defense allows the passes.
5. The second time through, defense tries to deny the passes.
6. When the three offensive players get to the three-point line at the opposite end, they are allowed to attack the basket. It is all-out three on three at that point.

Coaching Points

- Remind players to help and recover to the ball, putting pressure on each pass and dribble.
- Remind players to see their player and the ball.
- Don't allow the wing offensive players to get ahead of the ball.

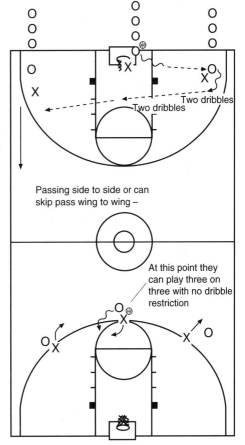

Passing side to side or can skip pass wing to wing –

At this point they can play three on three with no dribble restriction

DENY, OPEN, DENY

Pat Summitt | *University of Tennessee*

Purpose

To teach defenders wing denial and to open in the lane to see the ball and their player.

Organization

A defensive player, an offensive player, and a coach with a ball are on the wing. Another coach with a ball is on the other wing.

Procedure

1. The coach slaps the ball to begin the drill; the defender denies.
2. The offensive player tries to receive the ball at least twice by breaking out to the wing.
3. The offensive player goes to the basket, across the lane, and up to the right wing. The defender opens up her stance, fronts the offensive player across the lane then closes her stance, and denies the offense as she cuts to the right wing.

Coaching Points

- Have experienced coaches attempt to pass to the wing.
- Emphasize that the defender should play up the ball line.
- Have defenders react quickly when the offensive player makes her second cut up the wing to receive the ball.

Variation

On the second attempt to receive the ball on the right wing, the coach attempts a pass that the defender can steal or knock down.

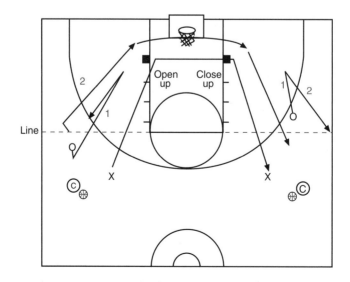

165   DENY THE BALL, TAKE THE CHARGE

Lisa Bluder | *University of Iowa*

Purpose

To work on denial defense and on getting to the weakside position on the pass, helping on the drive, and taking the charge.

Organization

Use a minimum of three players, one coach, and two balls. A manager is helpful.

Procedure

1. The coach begins the drill positioned on one side of the top of the key.
2. An offensive player is on the strong side, and another is on the weak side.
3. One defensive player denies the pass from the coach on the strong side.
4. The strongside offensive player tries to get open on one side of the floor. The coach throws the pass. Defense knocks the pass away and stays in denial position.
5. The coach passes the second ball to the weak side. The defense moves on the pass to a good weakside position.
6. The offensive player with the ball drives. Defense stops the drive and takes the charge outside of the paint.

Coaching Points

- Make sure the defense waits until the offense passes the second ball before moving to the weakside position.
- A manager can chase the balls that are knocked away.
- Stress good defensive movements.
- Teach players how to take the charge by absorbing the contact and landing safely.

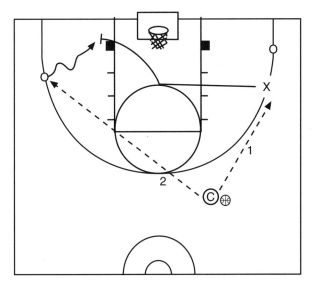

HELP AND RECOVER TO THREE-ON-THREE LIVE

Kay Yow | *North Carolina State University*

Purpose

To teach players to help and recover with proper defensive rotations.

Organization

Use six players, one coach, and one manager. Players are positioned in shell defense spots (offense and defense in both corners and offense and defense on the right wing). The coach is on the left wing, with two balls, and the manager is under the basket. Players rotate from offense to defense.

Procedure

1. The coach passes to O_1. On the pass, defensive players adjust (see figure 1).
2. Player O_1 passes to O_2. Again, the defensive players adjust (see figure 2).
3. The ball is skip-passed back to the coach. The coach drives right, requiring X_1 to help stop penetration. The coach then drives left, requiring X_3 to help stop penetration (see figure 3).
4. The coach passes to O_3, who penetrates the baseline. For the sake of the drill, X_3 allows O_3 to beat her (see figure 4).
5. On the penetration, X_2 slides over to help, and X_1 drops.
6. Player O_3 tries to pass across the baseline to O_2. Player X_1 knocks the ball out of bounds to the manager, and the coach throws a live ball to O_1.
7. Play is live three on three.

Coaching Points

- Players should develop good communication.
- Players should give early help and recover quickly.
- Players helping must have good body position to prevent the coach from getting to the basket. If the body position is open, the coach will have a direct path to the basket.
- Help on the baseline should occur outside the lane line; otherwise it will arrive too late.
- The ball needs to move quickly. This should be a fast-paced, intense drill.

Variation

Trap the ball handler on the baseline.

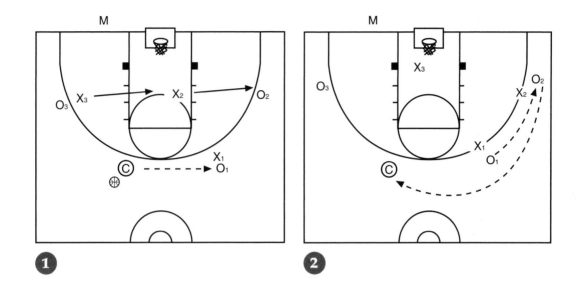

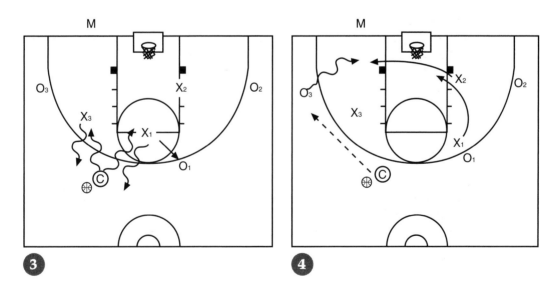

Nikki Caldwell | *University of Tennessee*

Purpose

To help players defend penetration and get to the helpside position.

Organization

Four players, two offense and two defense, are on the perimeter. A line of players is on each wing. The rotation moves offense to defense, defense out, and new offense comes in. The coach has a ball and will be a passer at the top.

Procedure

1. The defense denies passes to the wings.
2. As the coach passes to one side, the weakside defender rotates into helpside defense. Defensive players go to the middle of the lane (see figure 1).
3. To reverse the ball, players either pass to the coach, who reverses the ball, or they use a skip pass to the opposite wing.
4. The defense moves from helpside defense to on-ball defense (see figure 2).
5. Players come out in a stance with their feet moving to force the offense to the baseline. They should not let the offensive player come back to the middle.
6. The other defender becomes the helpside defense.

Coaching Points

- The player must get off to the help side.
- When the ball is reversed, the player comes out to defend in a defensive stance, with feet moving.
- Players should have active hands and force the offensive player to the baseline. They should keep penetration out of the middle of the court.

Variation

Once the weakside player recovers, let the defender get beat, and have the helpside defender rotate over and take the charge.

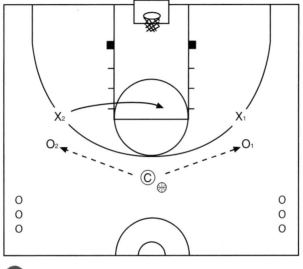

1

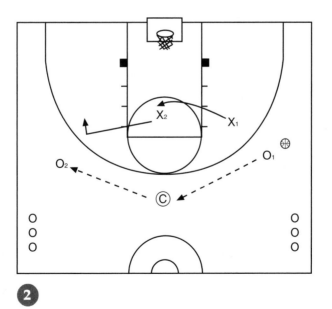

2

chapter 15

Post Drills

How should your players defend someone like Lisa Leslie? Should they play behind or in front? Should they sag or apply pressure? It's a tough call. Thankfully, not every post defender is as challenging, yet knowing what your defensive philosophy dictates will guide your players in determining how to best stop a top post player.

As in all defensive approaches, your choice of positioning will affect not only the post players, but also their perimeter teammates. Pressuring intensely on the wings may make passing inside more difficult, and fronting on the low post requires active and conscientious weakside help. Building your players' confidence and sense of team concept is essential if you are to realize your defensive intentions.

Defending Lisa Leslie isn't a challenge most coaches will face, but there are certainly other opponents who will present a formidable test. Learn from the following coaches what makes their post defenders exceptional, and your players will face any opponent of any size with confidence and poise.

TWO-ON-TWO IN THE POST

Lisa Bluder | *University of Iowa*

Purpose

To work on defending the post from the weakside defense and from the post-to-post screen.

Organization

Use two offensive posts; two defensive posts; three coaches, managers, or passers; and one ball.

Procedure

1. The offensive and defensive players are in the low post area.
2. The passers are at the top of the key and at each wing. One of the passers passes the ball into the post.
3. The offense can post, flash to high post, or screen away.
4. The defense works on proper positioning for post defense.
5. The defense goes to offense, and a new defense steps in on every third possession.

Coaching Points

- Get weakside posts off their players and moving so they can't be effectively screened.
- Encourage defensive players to talk and communicate on all screens.

Variation

The defensive posts stay on defense until they get a steal or rebound.

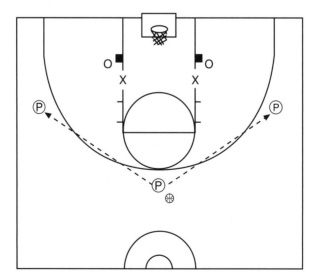

ONE-ON-ONE POST

Lisa Bluder | *University of Iowa*

Purpose
To work on the reactions of offensive and defensive post players.

Organization
Use one offensive and one defensive post, one coach, and one ball.

Procedure
1. The two posts are along the lane facing away from the coach, who is near the low-block area.
2. The coach has a ball and calls the name of either post.
3. The called player becomes the offense and the other becomes the defense.
4. The offensive player flashes to the strong side to receive the ball, and the defensive player reacts to play defense against her.

Coaching Points
- Players should move quickly to receive the pass, remembering to put up a target hand and call for the ball.
- Defenders should use good hustle and footwork to deny the pass, or use good block-out footwork to allow just one shot by the offense.

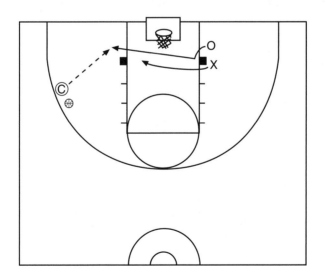

LOW-POST PIT

Lisa Bluder | *University of Iowa*

Purpose
To work on low-post defensive footwork and positioning.

Organization
Use four passers, one offensive player, one defender, and one ball.

Procedure
1. Four passers are at the three-point line in typical shell positions.
2. One offensive player and one defender work at the low post area.
3. The passers pass the ball around to each other until they can cleanly pass the ball into the post.
4. If the offensive post player receives a pass, she makes a move to the basket to score. Defenders box out and outlet to a passer.
5. Continue the drill for one minute. Rotate positions.

Coaching Points
- Don't allow lob passes because there is no help for the defender.
- Make sure the post offense stays active in trying to get open for the ball.
- Review and teach all possible defensive post positions according to where the ball is.
- Keeping score for each player makes the drill more competitive.

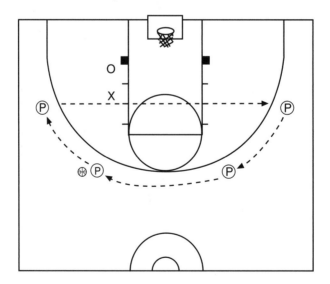

POST DEFENSE

Theresa Grentz | *University of Illinois*

Purpose

To prevent the pass into the post player.

Organization

One offensive player is at the top of the key, one is on each wing, and one is in the low post on one side. The defender assumes a position on the post based on where the ball starts in the drill.

Procedure

1. Players on the perimeter pass the ball to each other.
2. The offensive post player (O_1) is free to move to any position within the free throw lane. The defensive player (X_1) must remain in a good defensive position and attempt to deny the pass into the post.

Coaching Point

The defensive post player should beat the offense to where she wants to post up.

Variation

Work on anticipating the post player's cuts and using proper footwork to reestablish denial defense.

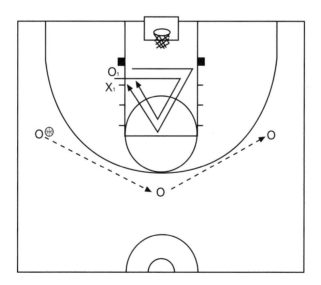

Theresa Grentz | *University of Illinois*

Purpose
To teach a denial-position pass from a wing or the corner to the post.

Organization
One offensive player is on the block, one on the wing, and one in the corner; one defensive player is on the wing or corner, and the other is in the post.

Procedure
1. Player X_1 pressures the ball when it is either on the wing or in the corner.
2. Player X_2 denies the pass into the post by playing position defense (depending on where the ball is).
3. If the pass is made into the post, X_1 collapses to assist the post defender.
4. When offense passes the ball out from the post, X_1 goes to pressure the ball.

Coaching Points
- The post defender should step up and deny the entry pass. Players should always have a hand in the passing lane regardless of the ball position. This requires the defense to beat the offense to spots on the floor and see the ball at all times.
- The wing or corner defender must attack the ball. She can also double down on the offensive post player to force the ball back out to the wing or the corner.

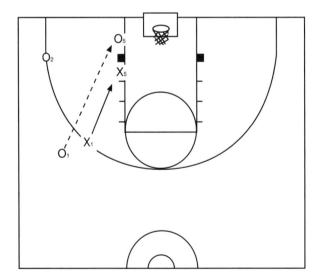

FIVE-POINT CLOSEOUT

Jon Newlee | *Idaho State University*

Purpose

To simulate defensive closeouts from the help position and work on defending the backdoor cut. To teach the basic footwork and fundamentals for defending on the closeout and backdoor cut. To improve conditioning.

Organization

With cones or basketballs, mark five spots on the floor outside the three-point line: two in the corners on the baseline, two on the wings, and one at the top of the key. One player starts under the basket, and the rest of the team lines up along the baseline.

Procedure

1. On the whistle, X_1 sprints to her left to the first cone and closes out. Her top foot and hand (right foot and hand on the first two cones and left foot and hand on the last two cones) should be slightly in front, forcing the offensive player to have to go baseline. On the cone at the top of the key, the coach designates which direction to force the offensive player.
2. Once X_1 has started the drill, X_2 steps in under the basket. She should be ready to go in a defensive stance, simulating help defense.
3. After closing out, X_1 quickly snaps her head around to the inside (looking over her inside shoulder), keeping her back toward the top of the key, and puts her hand nearest the basket up in the passing lane and shuffles toward the middle of the key. This simulates taking away the backdoor cut.
4. When X_1 reaches the paint, after defending the backdoor, she turns and sprints to close out at the next cone. When she reaches the second cone, X_2 sprints to close out at the first cone, and the next person steps under the basket. Continue this sequence until the last player finishes the drill.
5. Players can start the drill in the opposite direction, with X_1 sprinting to her right to close out.

Coaching Points

- Emphasize keeping the hands up and making small, quick steps, or "squeaking your feet," as the defender reaches the cone on the closeout. The defender's hands should be high enough to take away passing lanes and to contest shots.
- Remind players to look over their inside shoulder when defending the backdoor cut instead of looking at the ground or where they are going.
- Emphasize quick changes of direction.

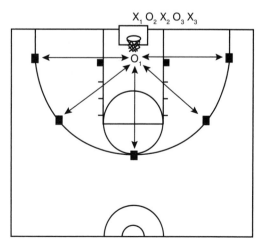

174 TWO-ON-TWO REBOUND WITH CLOSEOUT

Wes Moore | *University of Tennessee at Chattanooga*

Purpose
To stress the importance of closing out to the shooter, making contact, and sliding to maintain inside position in the lane without getting pushed under the basket.

Organization
A line of players is at each elbow, and a line of players is on each side of the lane along the baseline.

Procedure
1. The first person in each line at the elbows are partners on offense, while the first person in each line on the baseline are partners on defense.
2. One of the defensive players starts with the ball and passes to one of the offensive players (see figure 1).
3. Each defender closes out to the offensive player on her side of the lane.
4. The offensive player with the ball shoots, and both offensive players crash the boards (see figure 2). Continue play on a make or a miss.
5. The defenders try to use an arm-bar on their opponent to slow them, then reverse pivot to a box-out position.
6. Whoever controls the rebound becomes the offense and tries to score. There is no out of bounds and contact is allowed. Because it's a battle for the rebound, the shooter must go up strong.
7. Play continues until someone scores or until the offense stops attacking. Then players rotate, with the team that scores going to the baseline, and the team that loses going to the elbows.

Coaching Points
- The defender should close out to the offensive player and initiate face-to-face contact. They should not wait on the offense to come to them and deliver the blow, but rather should go out to claim more ground.
- The defender should pivot and get the offense on her back, slide to maintain inside position, and stay low and wide to avoid getting pushed under the basket.
- Once the player knows where the ball will come off the rim, she should release and fly to the ball.
- The offensive player should be strong with the ball and finish against contact. Players who maintain the inside position on the box-out should be rewarded with an easy put-back.

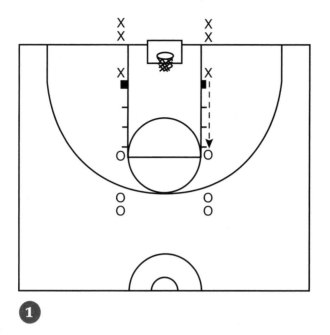

1

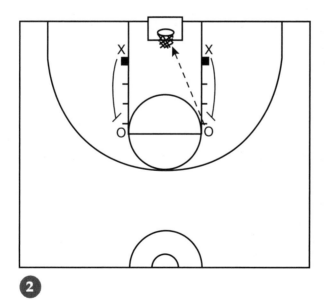

2

Wes Moore | *University of Tennessee at Chattanooga*

Purpose

To work on the technique and execution of the drop-step post move, sealing the defense on the inside shoulder.

Organization

A ball is located on each side of the lane just above the block. A coach is under the basket, a coach or manager is at each elbow, and one offensive player is on the block.

Procedure

1. The player starts in a post-up position on the block, with the ball on the floor in front of her.
2. The player picks up the ball and chins it, then glances over her inside shoulder as if to read the defense.
3. She whips her outside leg toward the rim while using a power dribble to get to the basket (see figure 1).
4. The player gathers herself and goes up strong off two feet for the layup.
5. The player then flashes across the lane and repeats the procedure on the other side (see figure 2). A coach or manager replaces the balls back on the block for the duration of the drill.

Coaching Points

- The player should be sitting low, with her elbows out and hands up (thumbs pointed toward ears) ready for a big post-up.
- Players should drop-step with their feet pointed toward the basket and slam the dribble down with two hands out in front of them.

Variations

- Put a dummy defense on the player so she can work on sealing the defense with her leg and scoring against contact.
- Use different low-post moves on the block.

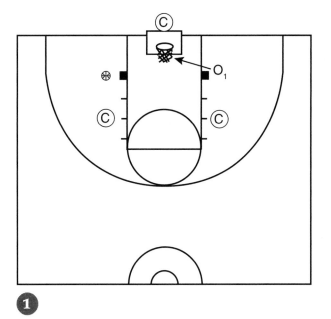

1

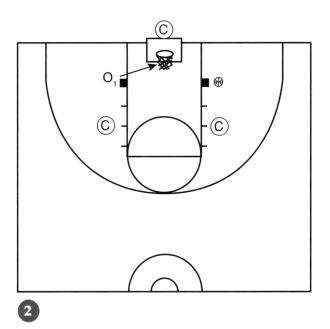

2

FOUR PASSES

Rene Portland | *Penn State University*

Purpose

To improve a post player's ability to run the floor while also working on a guard's ability to pass the ball ahead in transition.

Organization

Three players use one ball. The guards form two lines, one at the extended foul line (out of bounds) in the backcourt and the other at the hash mark in the front-court. Post players form a line on the elbow in the backcourt on the same side as the guards.

Procedure

1. The first post player in line tosses the ball off of the backboard and secures the rebound. The player then outlets the ball to the guard on her end of the court.
2. The guard passes the ball to the second guard at the far end of the court.
3. After outletting the ball, the post player sprints the floor looking for a fast-break layup. Meanwhile, the guard dribbles into position to make a good entry pass to the post (see figure 1).
4. The guard can either pass to the post player on the fly, or the post player can establish post-up position and receive the pass from the guard.
5. On the shot, the guard runs to the middle of the lane to establish rebounding position.
6. After scoring, the post player takes the ball out of bounds. The guard moves to the outlet spot on the opposite side of the floor.
7. The post player inbounds the ball to the guard and sprints the floor (see figure 2).
8. The guard takes a few dribbles then passes ahead to the post player. The post player finishes the play with an uncontested layup.
9. The post player then moves to the end of the post line with a new post player initiating the drill. The guard goes to the end of the backcourt line, with the other guard moving to the frontcourt line.

Coaching Points

- The post player should know where the ball is at all times.
- The guard, on the return trip down the floor, should pass to the post player just after the post player has crossed half-court.

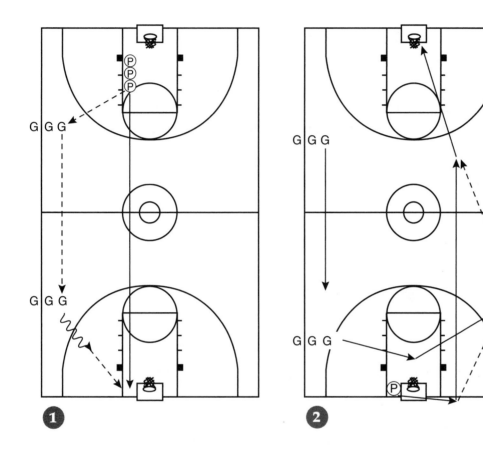

chapter 16

Team Drills

The Houston Comets' four WNBA titles speak volumes for the concept of team defense. Sure, they had terrific post players in Cynthia Cooper and Sheryl Swoopes, but most of all they have shown repeatedly that they can play team defense against anyone.

How does a team of exceptional athletes (or perhaps not so exceptional athletes) perform at such an impressive level? Getting your players to make a defensive commitment and to play intensely without faltering over time is a goal many coaches share but few have been able to accomplish.

The final chapter in this book provides drills to help put the *team* in your defensive approach. The fundamentals of footwork, rebounding, perimeter and post pressure, screen management, and transition defense will give your players the knowledge and confidence to play against their opponents on any night. Demanding your players' focus, attention, and unselfishness may make the same difference that has separated the Houston Comets from the rest of the WNBA.

THREE SCREENS (FOUR-ON-FOUR)

Andy Landers | *University of Georgia*

Purpose

To practice setting and defending three types of screens in a game situation.

Organization

Four offensive players and four defensive players align on the wings and blocks. One coach has a ball.

Procedure

1. The coach has the ball at the top and starts dribbling to the right. Player O_1 down screens for O_2 (see figure 1).
2. After screening down, O_1 flash pivots back to the dribbler for one count, then block-to-block screens for O_3 (see figure 2).
3. After the block-to-block screen takes place, the coach dribbles across the top to the left, then O_1 back screens for O_4.
4. The coach dribbles back to the right, and O_2 starts to down screen.

Coaching Points

- Emphasize setting good, legal screens.
- Use the screens effectively; set your player up and make crisp cuts.

Variation

After everyone goes through all three screens, pass the ball to someone who is open and play four on four.

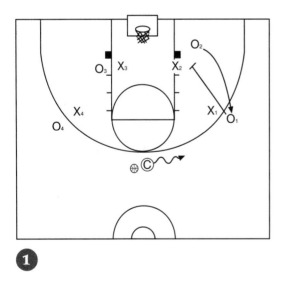

FIVE-ON-FOUR

Tim Shea | *Salem State College*

Purpose

To prevent open shots and to rotate to defend open opponents.

Organization

Use five offensive players against four defensive players, one ball, and half the court.

Procedure

1. Offense must make two perimeter passes before shooting or passing inside.
2. The defense always rotates to the ball and does not cover the player farthest from the ball.
3. The ball handler (O_1) is always covered, along with the next two closest offensive players (O_2 and O_3). Player X_4 watches the remaining two offensive players, O_4 and O_5. She defends whichever one is the most dangerous (see figure 1).
4. When the ball reaches O_4 (see figure 2), X_4 must sprint to defend O_4. Player X_3 drops to defend X_5. Player X_2 remains on O_2 while X_1 drops into a zonelike position as she awaits movement into a scoring area by either O_1 or O_3.

Coaching Points

- Have the defense move to offense when they stop the offense from scoring three times in a row. Do not consider a foul as stopping the offense. Continue the count.
- Don't allow the four defenders to play a zone. They must cover someone. Only one defender is in a zonelike position at any one time.
- Remind players not to give up a shot to anyone, and that they should leave their player to defend the open player if they have to.

Variation

Play four on three.

1

2

FIVE-ON-FIVE SHELL

Wendy Larry | *Old Dominion University*

Purpose

To work on defensive help positioning on the perimeter and work on communication.

Organization

Five offense players spread out around the perimeter, and five defense players match up. One of the offensive players has the ball.

Procedure

1. Defense has three positions—on ball, denial, and help. On ball is when the offensive player has the ball, denial is when the offensive player is one pass away, and help is when the offensive player is two or three passes away. The farther the offensive player is from the ball, the farther the defender can be from her player.
2. The offensive player with the ball makes a pass (see figure 1). The receiver holds the ball at least three seconds before passing so the defense has the opportunity to get in good position, and the coach has an opportunity to make corrections if someone is out of position. Offense must hold the ball and cannot dribble or shoot (see figure 2).
3. Repeat step 2 until the defense knows where they should be and are getting there. Switch offense and defense.

Coaching Points

- Make sure defense moves on the release of a pass and that they don't stand and watch, then react late.
- Even though players perform this drill in almost slow motion, don't let the defense slack. Make sure they get in correct position quickly. Approach to the ball is important.
- When the offensive player at the top of the key receives the ball, emphasize that if she is in the middle of the court, there is no help. Tell the defender to force her to a side.

Variation

After your team has learned proper positioning, allow the offense to play live. Give them rules (e.g., only two dribbles, no screens, no shooting until 10 passes are made, no outside shots). This is a positioning drill to teach and review basic concepts.

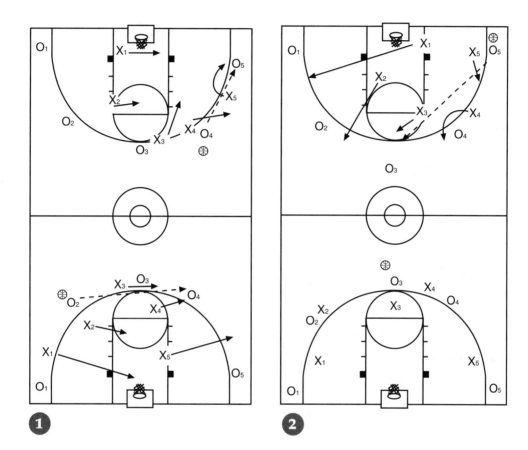

David Smith | *Bellarmine University*

Purpose

To teach defensive players how to defend each type of screen or cut. In this continuous drill, players defend a down screen, back screen, cross screen, pick-and-roll, shuffle cut, and pick-the-picker situation and deny cutters.

Organization

Use six players (three on offense and three on defense), one coach, and one ball. Station additional players off the court, ready to rotate in.

Procedure

1. Begin the drill with O_1 in the point position, O_3 in the low post, and O_2 at the wing. Defense matches up accordingly.
2. The drill begins with a down screen, then flows continuously to a UCLA cut, pick-and-roll, deny cutters, deny the high-post cutter, back screen, cross screen, and pick-the-picker. The coach is on the side of the court that the drill begins on (see figures 1-8).
3. When the teams have completed the sequence of defensive situations, the offensive players leave the court, the defensive players become the offense, and three new defensive players come onto the court.

Coaching Points

- Emphasize communication, such as calling out screens, ball, shot, and so on, the little things you want your players to do on defense.
- You may prefer to defend some situations differently; adjust how the players defend each situation according to your defensive philosophy.
- In the beginning, teach defensive techniques and how you want your team to defend each situation. When you are confident that your players understand and can execute each defensive strategy, play the drill live.

Variation

In teaching, make each situation a two-on-two drill, with you as a passer or receiver as necessary, before going to the full sequence of situations.

1

2

3

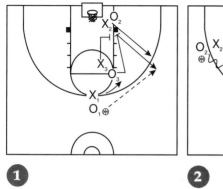

4

5

6

7

8

DEFENDING CUTTERS

Nikki Caldwell | *University of Tennessee*

Purpose
To help players recognize and defend cuts to the ball.

Organization
Two offensive players are on the wings, one with a ball, and one offensive player is inside. Three defensive players match up.

Procedure
1. The ball starts on the wing opposite the player inside. The weakside defenders on the post and on the wing get to helpside defense (see figure 1).
2. The weakside post cuts to the high post.
3. The post defense steps up and cuts the cutter in the lane. The post defenders aggressively deny.
4. The offensive post player (O_3) relocates to a ballside block. Post defense (X_3) defends the move by keeping the offensive player behind her, but staying in a denial stance (see figure 2).
5. The ball is reversed to the weakside wing (O_2) by a skip pass. The weakside defense goes from help side to defending the ball. Player X_2 comes out in a stance with her feet moving.
6. The defense (X_1) jumps to the helpside position. The weakside wing (O_1) flashes to the ball. The helpside defense defends that cut to the ball. The offensive player reads and then goes either to the top of the key after the cut or to a ballside block (see figure 3).
7. The defender sends the offensive player behind her if the cut is made to the block.

Coaching Points
- Players should cut the cutter and force her away from the basket or behind the defender.
- The offense should not cut in front of the defender.
- On the skip pass, the defense will have to get off to the helpside position.

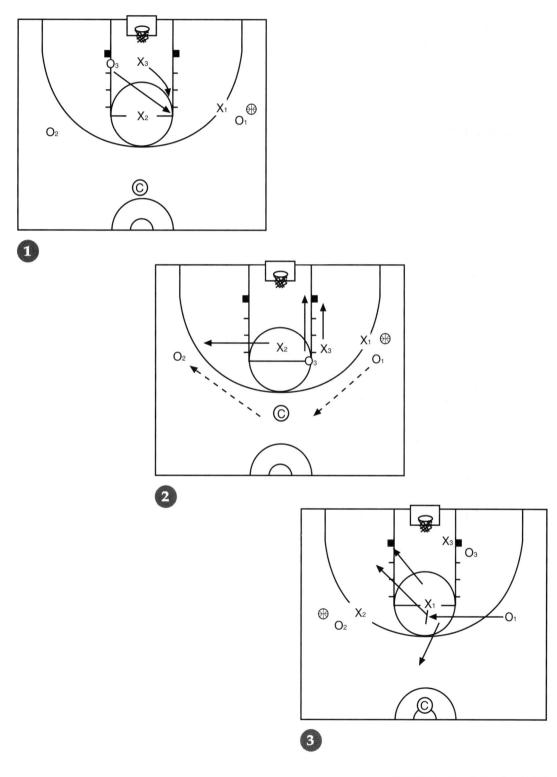

FOUR OUT FRONT (TRANSITION DEFENSE)

Amy Ruley | *North Dakota State University*

Purpose

To teach players to communicate with teammates in transition, with the defense focusing on positioning and player matchups during rotation.

Organization

Offensive players are in four lines on the end line, four defensive players are at the free throw line extended facing the end line, and one manager serves as an outlet.

Procedure

1. A manage or coach throws the ball to any one of the four offensive players. (The example here is with O_4.)
2. Player O_4 begins dribbling up the court, looking to pass ahead to teammates filling the lanes in a fast break.
3. Player X_4 sprints and touches the end line before joining teammates in a transition defense (see figure 1).
4. The three other defensive players rotate and match up according to the ball position and offensive player movement.
5. The drill is finished when the offensive team scores or the defense creates a turnover or rebounds a missed shot and outlets to the manager on the sideline. Players rotate from offense to defense, the defense goes out, and a new set of offensive players comes in from the end line.

Coaching Points

- Players should stop the ball. The defensive players closest to the ball adjust to the offensive player.
- Players must communicate. They should talk and point to locate the ball while sprinting and backpedaling to match up.
- The offensive team spreads across the floor to challenge defensive spacing.

Variations

- Defense faces the opposite end line and sprints three hard steps, pivots, and locates the ball.
- Players follow fast-break principles or make a patterned break.
- Both offensive and defensive teams circle around the coach, who shoots a basket. A matchup and rebound outlet sequence follow (see figure 2).

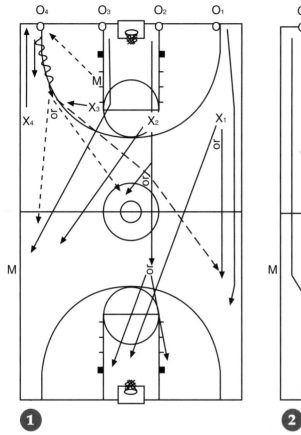

1

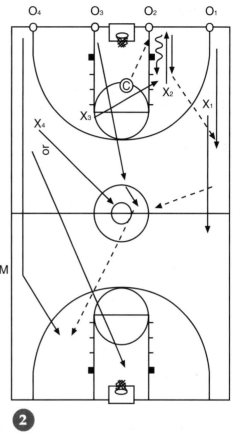

2

Nancy Winstel | *Northern Kentucky University*

Purpose

To teach proper defensive positioning for on-ball, denial (one pass away), and helpside situations. To teach the defense how to defend ball screens and screens away from the ball. To help players learn how to make a strong cut, how to set and use screens, and how to find the open person.

Organization

Three offensive players, one with a ball, and three defensive players are at half-court. Additional groups of three are ready to substitute in (you can also use groups of four with one substitute). Players rotate offense to defense and defense out.

Procedure

1. The drill begins at half-court with the offensive players keeping the ball alive, setting good ball screens, using the screens, and making good cuts.
2. The defense puts pressure on the ball to force it to the sideline and tries to remain active (see figure 1). If the ball is picked up, defense is in full-pressure defense. If a ball screen occurs, the defense moves toward their players and goes over the top of the screen.
3. Players may switch (see figures 2 and 3).

Coaching Points

- Stop the drill as necessary to make sure that players are calling out screens and calling out help.

Variations

- Run this drill initially at the half-court area facing the basket, without taking shots. Focus on pressuring the ball, pressuring the passing lanes, defending screens on and off the ball, and playing good help defense.
- Have the defense play until they get a steal or until the 30-second clock expires.
- Allow offensive players to shoot, drive, and post.
- Have the players switch on all screens. Defense steps out when switching, pressuring the ball hard.

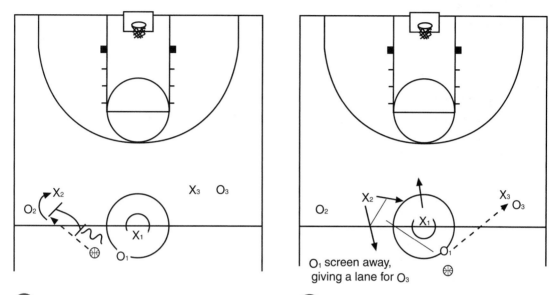

1

2

O₁ screen away,
giving a lane for O₃

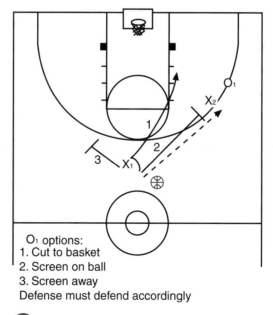

O₁ options:
1. Cut to basket
2. Screen on ball
3. Screen away
Defense must defend accordingly

3

POST DEFENSIVE DRILL WITH HELP

Nancy Winstel | *Northern Kentucky University*

Purpose

To teach proper defensive positioning in the post. To teach movement, intensity, communication with teammates, concentration, eye–hand coordination, and working in a confusing situation.

Organization

Three offensive players and three defensive players form a triangle in or near the lane. Four players are passers on the perimeter; one has a ball. Two coaches are on the court; each has a ball.

Procedure

1. The offensive players inside stay in their positions and don't move much. They should catch the ball if it is passed to them, but then they should pass it back out to a coach. The defensive-post players do all the work, which involves reacting to the ball on the perimeter and blocking passes from coaches (see figure 1).
2. To start the drill, the perimeter players pass a ball to each other; they may make skip passes or direct passes. Even though other balls will be moving, this ball determines the position that the defense plays in relationship to their offensive players. This ball is never passed inside.
3. The coaches pass to the inside, one ball at a time and only when the perimeter ball is on that side. The defense moves quickly, retrieves the ball, and immediately returns the ball to the coach. The drill moves fast, balls are flying, and players are moving (see figure 2).
4. The drill is complete when the players have played defense at all three spots.

Coaching Points

- Keep the drill active by having the perimeter players move the ball quickly.
- Remind the defense to talk and move throughout the drill.
- Make all types of passes: chest, bounce, lobs, roll the ball, and so on, while constantly checking to make sure the defense is in proper position.

Variation

As the ball moves along the perimeter, call "shot," and have the defensive players turn and box.

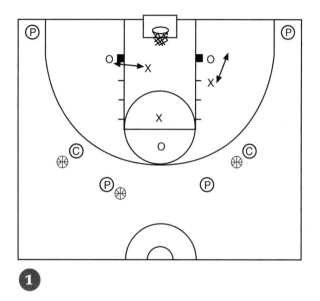

1

2

TRIANGLE REBOUNDING
(PERIMETER SERIES)

Nancy Winstel | *Northern Kentucky University*

Purpose

To teach proper box-out techniques, defensive positioning techniques for perimeter players, and the fundamentals of the fast break.

Organization

Use three defensive players, three offensive players, two coaches, and a ball. A manager is ready with another ball.

Procedure

1. Three offensive and three defensive players form a triangle. The coaches pass the ball with one another and with defensive players who are in proper defensive position (see figure 1).
2. Coaches may also dribble with penetration. The defense stops the ball (see figure 2).
3. After moving the ball quickly back and forth, a coach shoots, and the defensive players go to their offensive players, make good contact on the box-out, and get the ball. After a defender secures the rebound, she outlets the ball to a teammate.
4. The play continues with the defenders filling their lanes as they run to half-court. Meanwhile, the first offensive team goes to defense, and three new players come in on offense. The manager with the second ball quickly gives the ball to the coach so that the drill is continuous. The drill moves quickly.

Coaching Points

- Move the drill quickly and demand intensity from players. Players should make contact on all box-outs.
- If the shot is made and offense gets the rebound, play three-on-three until the goal is made or until the defense secures a rebound. If offense makes a basket, the defense quickly inbounds the ball and looks for a transition.

Variations

- Pass to a wing offensive player. The player beats her defender to the baseline. Defense calls for help, and help stops the ball. The top slides down, and the player who got beat slides up to box out the offensive player. The player who drove the baseline takes a jump shot (see figure 3).
- Offense keeps the drive, and help takes charge. Everyone else on defense rotates and boxes out an offensive player (see figure 4).

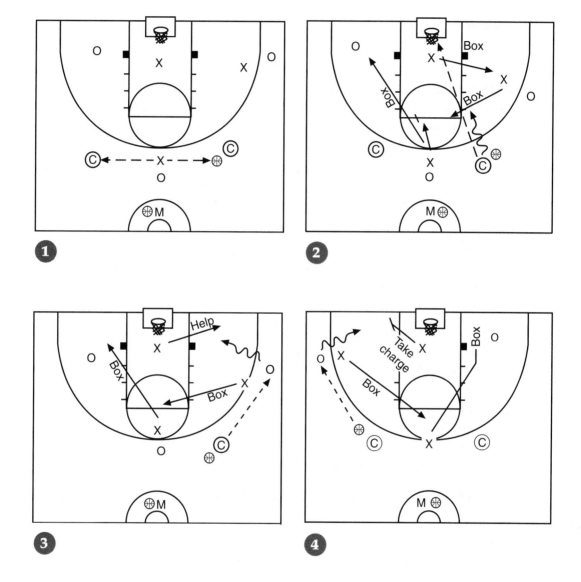

Nancy Winstel | *Northern Kentucky University*

Purpose

To teach proper rebounding box-out techniques, proper post defensive positioning, communication, intensity, and the beginning of the fast break.

Organization

Use three offensive players, three defensive players, two passers, two coaches, and one ball.

Procedure

1. Players begin the drill with offense and defense in a triangle in the post area. Two passers are on the baseline (see figure 1).
2. One coach has the ball. The coaches pass to each other, checking proper defensive positioning throughout the drill (see figure 2). The coaches can dribble to make the defense react.
3. After a few passes, one coach shoots the ball. The players make contact on the box, and then go get the rebound.
4. After the defense controls the rebound, an outlet is made to a teammate and the break begins. Meanwhile, the first offensive team goes to defense, and three new players come in on offense. The drill moves quickly.

Coaching Points

- Move the drill quickly, demanding intensity from the players. Players must be physical during the drill.
- If the shot is made and offense gets the rebound, have players go three on three until the goal is made or until defense secures a rebound. If a player makes a basket, she quickly inbounds the ball.

Variations

- Pass to the wing. She passes to the post player on the block, who has beaten her player. The defense rotates to pick up and box out the shooter and the other offensive players (see figure 3).
- Players use the variation just described, but the help defense steps in and takes the charge. The other two defenders rotate and box out (see figure 4).

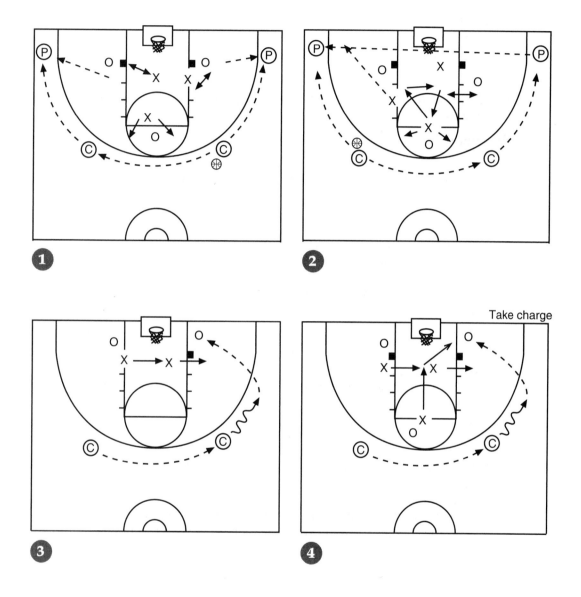

Take charge

About the WBCA

Founded in 1981, the **Women's Basketball Coaches Association (WBCA)** promotes women's basketball by unifying coaches at all levels to develop a reputable identity for the sport of women's basketball and fosters and promotes the development of the game in all of its aspects as a sport for women and girls.

With members throughout the world, it is the largest organization of its kind. The WBCA is involved in a variety of events and clinics throughout the year, including the WBCA High School All-America Game; the Betty F. Jaynes Internship Program; the Nike So You Want To Be A Coach Program and the annual WBCA National Convention, held in conjunction with the NCAA Women's Final Four. Through these events, the WBCA not only highlights exceptionally talented female players, but also provides opportunities for coaches at all levels to better themselves.

In addition to the activities that the WBCA puts on and sponsors, the organization has an extensive awards program through which the best, brightest, and most talented athletes, coaches, and contributors to women's basketball are honored. The WBCA also provides coverage on all aspects of women's basketball, from high school to the pros, through their three publications: *Coaching Women's Basketball*, *Net.News* and *Compliance Corner*.

For more information on these and the many activities and opportunities available from the WBCA, check out *www.wbca.org*.

Contributors

The following are coaches who contributed to *The Women's Basketball Drill Book*:

Jane Albright, Wichita State University
Gary Blair, Texas A&M University
Lisa Bluder, University of Iowa
Joan Bonvicini, University of Arizona
Beth Burns, San Diego State University
Nikki Caldwell, University of Tennessee
Jody Conradt, University of Texas
Leslie Crane, Western Illinois University
Kathy Delaney-Smith, Harvard University
Elaine Elliott, University of Utah
Nancy Fahey, Washington University
Brenda Frese, University of Maryland
Mike Geary, Michigan State University
Bill Gibbons, College of the Holy Cross
Brian Giorgis, Marist College
Cindy Griffin, Saint Joseph's University
Chris Gobrecht, Yale University
Carey Green, Liberty University
Theresa Grentz, University of Illinois
Mary Hegarty, Long Beach State University
Bonnie Henrickson, University of Kansas
Kris Huffman, Depauw University
Rick Insell, Middle Tennessee State University
Laurie Kelly, Northern Arizona University
Patrick Knapp, University of Pennsylvania
Andy Landers, University of Georgia
Wendy Larry, Old Dominion University
Bob Lindsay, Kent State University

Chris Long, Louisiana Tech University
John Margaritis, University of California at Riverside
Bernadette Mattox, WNBA's Connecticut Sun
April McDivitt, University of California at Santa Barbara
Muffet McGraw, University of Notre Dame
Joe McKeown, George Washington University
Wes Moore, University of Tennessee-Chattanooga
Jon Newlee, Idaho State University
Trina Patterson, University of Albany
Rene Portland, Penn State University
Gordy Presnell, Boise State University
Carol Ross, University of Mississippi
Julie Rousseau, Pepperdine University
Amy Ruley, North Dakota State University
Debbie Ryan, University of Virginia
Tim Shea, Salem State College
David Smith, Bellarmine University
Barbara Stevens, Bentley College
Pat Summitt, University of Tennessee
Ed Swanson, Sacred Heart University
Charlene Thomas-Swinson, University of Tulsa
Tara VanDerveer, Stanford University
Christina Wielgus, Dartmouth College
Nancy Winstel, Northern Kentucky University
Kay Yow, North Carolina State University

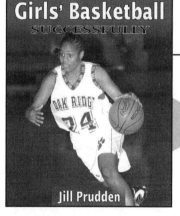